Library of Congress Cataloging-in-Publication Data Gumpel, Zachary.

Prem/ Zachary Gumpel.-1st ed.

ISBN-13:
978-0615553481

Printed in The United States of America

For more info please visit: PremTheBook.com

A lack of inside numbers on the ear,
with a margin just as dear.

i

To the people
Who change
Revolution in the midst

Discuss words in your words at Premthebook.com

i

Table of Contents

Chapter 6. Fallings

You are the king said the kids in the yard. You are the king as you cast your last card. Bent past sky's last star, woven thick between the ranges of the ever- made mar. Wish. Wash. Wishy Whitman water wash. Walking clocked and ready mocking; buy me a dollar. We are the kings of the black blue empire.

Chapter 7. What side of the river

Asked he honestly: Are we atop the serpent's crown, or just mere mortals staring up, while we are standing down?
-A good life came and went and this and that destroyed the other.-
Finally when he looked upon the rest, he sadly said that we may never go, just beyond the crest, of this freshly corniced snow.

Chapter 8. Island Excessum

This purple blue breeze island implies my will's intention. Sweet Rhine dunes flutter off prose to over dined dimensions. Freak of vision, layers of view. A sweet ascension as the purple breeze comes blue.

Chapter 9. Lights sounds different

The fading cross to wave the tumbles Find her in these wading rumbles Through the fading wave that crumbles Find here in these something symbols The ending start of sounds to jumble

Chapter 10. These days

Beneath from where the blunders come, I rock and sway with patience. In the place from where the umber runs, I mock and play on salience. No more shall the slumber numb. - I rewind forgetful ailments .

i

Portraits of memory.

Chapter One

India has a box on its international customs form that offers pilgrimage as a reason for visiting. I suppose then that I thought the purpose of the visit to this land was tourism. So tourism I checked. I looked towards these bleak words before the dark man behind the pressure board desk and concluded that I have never liked the word tourism. Almost the Latin *tornare*, to circle around a central point, the terminal efficacy of etymology. I had made up my mind; I did not wish to make circles. From the baggage claim my father and I proceeded on to the drivers who stood ready and waiting for business. And although he felt like a superhero for bringing me to this place, we said nothing to one another as we surveyed the crowd for a friendly face with a newfound street sense. With a good man in our pocket we rode off for the city. I restlessly take to the page for sound.

Arid communications proliferating seconds,
Antioch nations fighting wealth wilted wretches,
Acrobatic indulgence filling paradigms galore;
vicious things these little mimes; - they do implore

I did not know to write, only a poem here and a poem there. The space before the words. But to admit that I do not know something is worth a certain amount of words in and of itself. What I presume to have thought speeding through the streets of Bangalore is something so far removed from my present truth that I do not know the thought. But in a way, if I dare describe it: My eighteen years owned me and I was soundly sleeping. I was sleeping then, and had been sleeping the entirety of my life. The pinnacle of this sleep was the moment I stepped into India. My father and I sat comfortably smiling as the city went by. The song *Father and Son* played about my mind; what a fucking cliché. You see, I deduce I was sleeping then, but perhaps I am sleeping now, only more soundly.

This is what I think, as I file through all the following thoughts that I shall present. And as for the words I achieve from others, I shall use what I feel they would have said if they had listened to their hearts. For it is only on the rare occasion that words mimic the truth by the person we know to be, alongside the persons we are not, but still they are all who we will always be. Meanderings. Although all writings of truth do end in strange farce, the most honest element even in the lie is the thought, and they, much like truths as I have already extrapolated, hardly exist in a tangible form. So back now to what has happened. I had nothing reserved and nothing to speak was on my mind. My father looked heavy in the eyes. Jet lag and culture shock sat me in a state of high. Being beaten and tired from spending all that I had makes me seem more alive. And then people out on the road. Orderly chaos, people all around buying and selling, buying and selling. Vagabonds all; humans, dogs, and cows, what were they all doing and what was I doing passing them in a paid cab? A retro Tata van.

My father got going on about how the place had changed since his last visit some sun-cycles before. I listened in and out to the no more bicycles, more auto rickshaws, and plenty more garbage from India's new relationship with the plastic bag talk. It all seemed pointless, but I enjoyed the thick sense these words seemed to produce. Time passed, much as a great many pages in a Tolstoy, maybe. We arrived. I set eyes on what looked to be a hotel, an old building with a colonial facade. Green ferns lined the path leading up to its dark entrance. Our driver hopped from the van and banged on the glass entrance with his fist. "Guests, G," the driver screamed. Quickly a thin man with almond colored skin emerged. He was barefoot and wore a red blazer with no undershirt, navy blue pants, and a fez cocked to the side of his miniature head. He smiled at us as we started for the doors.

A younger man dressed in similar attire silently carried away our bags as soon as we entered. In the center of the lobby floor where we stood lay two cloth mats. These men were sleeping moments before, dreaming perhaps, as I wished I had been, or had been as you see. I hold myself, I'm alright here, I softly murmured with poise. Soon the old man gently took us by the hands and led us up to our quarters on the third floor. A rusted key was handed over. The looming smell of cardamom carried by humid air was all about. Every move my father made seemed calculated as for me to see it. His projections implied that he demanded I know that he himself was a male role model, though he did not believe it. We entered a room made quite bare, giving loose interpretations of what things might be like. We organized our materials and got into our cots resting atop plywood frames. Relaxed, we spoke of our lives intersecting in such a place, and what India might be like tomorrow.

Morning came with perfumes of spices and sounds from people bustling in the streets below. "Good morning," my father said with his eyes still closed. "Good morning," I said looking out the porch window. "We'll need to lose ourselves as best we can here. Don't ignore what's happened with life, acknowledge it, disregard it as your own and progress with now as something that is never the same." He said this with airs of joke. A bit deep for the morning. I had always loved to ponder the life, but had almost lost the will to do so. I answered only with a nod and went for the shower. A cold water faucet with a bucket for pouring, shivers in the morning to wake the mind. This rid me of all tired, and made me feel as if I was doing something relevant. Downstairs we were to meet a few of our western friends who were staying in the same hotel. We had all planned to go to the Vishwa Shanti Ashram, where the job title is Master of Being, the open doors swinging in the winds. A collective community living in the creative conscience. A hermitage, an Eden by the hand of man.

Although the cold water had awakened me, I was dazed still from a few good years of hard drink and smoke and had little care of what happened. My life seemed without purpose. In fact, I wanted nothing to do with it, and regarded my time as lost. I knew it all and knew all to well. But today in a strange way it seemed as if I were giddy with staring eyes, as if I knew not a single possible outcome of the day nor of life. So we went for the dining hall, an unkempt grand room in an indoor courtyard within the hotel. We found a table and that same man who had taken us in the night before came with a bright and noble way and recited for us the foods offered."Ever since I was a young boy you've told me of India and your guru, you know, the smell of this place, about Rama Mata. You've described her as if she was your personification of love," I said.I knew only of India through dreamlike stories my father told me growing up. When my father would reminisce of his days here his entire face entertained a grin and his eyes kept enough of a story to keep me interested for years. "Yes, but it is all talk, I could never rightly explain the truth. I myself may never experience a thing," he hastily returned. All would soon reveal itself, two guys who were putting up a good fight to look as if they were really there. I started for the street and left my father sipping a coffee, figuring the exchange rate.

Outside amidst the colors, smokes, fruit vendors, and crowds of men going to work; carelessly, I strolled around with my hands tucked within my pants quietly whistling *Highway to Hell*. Embarrassed by my image in these streets I turned my head skyward wishing I were more like Thomas Mann's Felix Krull. I walked on farther, a man rode up beside me on his bicycle rickshaw. "A ride sir?" he asked. "I'm going no place at all, sir," I replied, and he laughed with his eyes. "Take time under consideration and be aware of time with as well as time without," I added. "Bang!" He shot me with a gun that he made with his fingers before pedaling off into the crowd. How homiletic of a street man; some fools of the wise just as much as the learned. Another bit of sugar to sprinkle on my mind.

My father called me over by the doors. He had located our friends Namadeve and Margalo along with a small tour they were guiding around. Associated with this group of tourists I felt like more of an animal, or maybe less of an animal and more like what some humans think they are. Only a short time before a drunk Chilean friend of mine described this scene as "gringo parade," the cliché white man with wide eyes and a closed mind when it came down to the grain. Yet, fuck, maybe I am and we are just more bastard clichés as well, maybe we're all on a gringo parade. A big ol' gringo parade. Namadeva, he was an American Hindu priest, and enough of lessons. He left his body not too long after I saw him and I never got to ask him what his remaining question was. Margalo, his wife, was a lawyer. The both of them were a good collection of modesty and masterful; they were the ones who organized the driver who was waiting out front.

In the van all us white people sat patiently awaiting our journey to take us. Namadeva threw the driver an address and he responded with a neck nod if it could be called this. It was the quintessential body language of India, and I did not see it first but rather understood the validity of the simple motion. Its significance is interchangeable and can mean yes or no and anything in between. I frowned at the fact that I knew no ownership of my obvious mannerisms but intended on realizing a good one. I am the character, but I could not then come to him. The car got off and sped on through the city swerving in and out of traffic. Only the car and the road, nothing else to muddy the waters like rules or painted lines.

Oh do tell us how to see the world, tell us you're not afraid.
Because I saw you when you left me, after you bade me that
advice.
You curled in your corner and chewed off all your skin.
You've lost your fucking mind wilting words where dénouement
begins.

We stopped the van on the side of a road. A psychologist and I spoke about experiences with LSD during intercourse and other such things like buying coffee at a cafe under the influence and the meaning of these things. The conquering of the intoxication and all the other perceptible elements. He claimed he was a master with the ladies, I could not see how. Off past a dirt road under construction rested a place that looked something like I imagined. Just beyond an embankment stood an off-white marble temple with a dirt path parallel leading down to some more temples and a four story statue of the Hindu mythological form, Vitala. Another path led to a gated entrance. A man in a white robe emerged from the temple to greet us. His face was smooth with small lips that smiled all by themselves. He was a Pujari, a priest; A god fearing man? I wondered. My father and Namadeva had recognized him from years before. The Pujari recognized Namadeva from his recent visit, and my father was remembered as well once he told him his spiritually given name: Devi Dass. "Sorry we are late," Namadeva said. "The Lunar calendar can be a wonder. It's really nothing, a day late, next year, today, and tomorrow," the Pujari said with a swivel of his head. It was the anniversary of the passing of a man my father defined as his guru, Keshavadas. The Pujari led us across the dirt path leading to a gate, unlatched it, and motioned for us to walk through and on down a ways until we reached the main house. The gates closed and the world of man changed face, its noise disappeared. Colors and the fragrance of flowers, sounds of birds and monkeys now overwhelmed the senses.

He'd perish dripping and drooling still in slighted steadfast gaze.
But for just a moment trees sway left; I lose my moot Malaise.

All the mouths lay still as we walked the path and came to the door of an old fifties-style home. Namadeva looked at us all with a straight approval and rang a classic turnkey bell. Slowly the door opened to reveal an elderly woman robed in an orange cloth, with long black hair that flowed down tired shoulders. Such an air of ease she had, like butterflies floating about the earth in their patternless sequence. Rama Mata, she greeted us with a slight bow pressing her hands together. She was an idol to my father and the others, but when I looked to her, I looked hard for the meaning the others seemed to not even seek but expect. I saw only a woman. She looked to my father and addressed him as if she had seen him only yesterday. She turned then to me and addressed me by a spiritual name, Prem Kumar. A name her husband gave me years before after seeing a picture from my youth. She hugged me wishing me welcome and invited us inside.

In the main room where we were led, commotion ran all around. Women carried foodstuffs through to the kitchen, men sat on the floor sipping chai. People walked around aimlessly looking toward the floor; I heard once that there is no money on the floor. Rama Mata sat us down but exclaimed that she had only a few moments to spare. The grounds demanded attention, the ceremonies and lunch were soon to take place. As she sat cross-legged before us each person made out a few questions in the form of inflected statements and directed them towards the feet of Rama Mata. I sat silently staring into her eyes testing in my own mind the concept of enlightenment and what it meant to be a person free from affected ideas and thoughts, to be one as the rest, but I could find nothing. The way she answered these child-like adults who had become as such in her presence even more so than they had acted before, was with simple eloquence as if each answer meant do not worry, all of the questions you have, have but all the same answers. With this I felt warm and confident that the inner voice had spoken truths, but why had we not listened? Do we never listen? Was it all so juxtaposed that even the double meaning could not be available to us? She rose and smiled, then started off back towards the kitchen, the whole of us stayed waiting for tea to arrive.

A well-fed servant lady of the lower class came round with a steaming chai for us each, and with mine I scanned the room. Two couches opposite each other covered in a red cashmere tapestry and an altar at the other end of the room with various deities within. Out of the blue Devi Dass caught me off guard, sternly whispering that I should try and get some time alone with Rama Mata when she was free. "Ask her questions about life and maybe for a new name," he said. Questions about general life seemed absurd. Life is such a place, isn't it? I am neither here nor there, so how could I ask about a name in my life when I did not even know who the fuck I was. I felt it was wrong to present this question. Who am I? No answer would suffice, nor did I have any attachments to my name, or to the irrelevance with which I held it. Prem Kumar, boy of cosmic love. People in the room spoke with one another, but they were silent under my thoughts. What was I doing here and why the fuck had I come? There was no party here, it was all customs, tradition, questions, answers. To the rescue; the ashram driver and confidence man Mahadeva entered the room with his daughter Anjana, a cute dark child who wore a white dress and silver bangles with bells at her ankles. She ran around the room greeting us strangers, prostrating to our feet.

For a moment I was taken by her and relieved myself from thought, but quickly returned. Mahadeva came off as such a wide-eyed fellow, as if all things intrigued him. The moment he walked into the room people began to move just a bit more. He enjoyed his effect. More talk went on about America and other things, people's stories of India, mythological jargon, but I could not hear them. My thoughts came in loud and distracted me from the scene. Left with my palate was a strong flavor of herbs and fresh milk taken that morning. A servant showed and took us with a nod down the hallway into the kitchen where vegetable heaps scattered across the floor. With their dark hands paper thin, women washed and cut them in preparation for lunch. Further along opened up a garage-like structure with tables and chairs in rows. On either side of the room wrought-iron gates led outside; a working woman bent from time with grayed out hair and eyes led us to the gate leading in the right direction.

The group went on before us as my father and I straggled behind. We walked a dirt path lined with palm trees and eucalyptus. Sitting in the red mud two bulls lay tied to a stake. I walked with my father. He was not himself. Giddy fear. Stalls for milking cows sprayed smells of manure into my journal. Some dogs yelled hungry from their own fear that men had left them behind. The path continued and let us off in a low-growth field and to our left stood a group of statues presenting us with the personifications of all seven auspicious rivers of India. *What time is it? Is this why we must masquerade with Britannicas?* The Ganga, Godavari, Narmada, Kaveri, Krushna, Brahmaputra, and Yamuna. Back a ways stood an eight-sided temple, a two-story horse drawn chariot guarded its entrance; a depiction of Krishna and Arjuna moments before battle; a scene from the Bagavad Gita; the picture of man, and beside him, his true self preparing for the collision with manifest illusion. In the far right corner of the plot was a most humble building, Mahasamati meditation mandir was written across the front in big red letters. Processions of people dressed in classic garb made their way inside singing songs in Sanskrit and Rama Mata's native tongue, Conquini. My father and I merged with the group and did our best to sing along. Like moments passing flowers in air absent of wind. I was alone there in my own procession of ponderous stride, as I imagine we are alone always, even within the altogether altruistic experience.

They see it as it runs down along those rocks with moss
This smaller flat begins to drown her song beneath the grass
But when the dunes across the way belonged to them at last
they were marooned as they were wrong to breeze this final
bending mast

      Crowds sit cross-legged on the floor without a thought
of difference. Men and women separate to either side of the
room. The roles of sex tremble the heart, yet all are equally
caught by the altar, a statue of Keshavadas sitting in the lotus
posture atop a grand looking chair upholstered in red leather. As
if we could ever be separate. To be not as you were , only if you
had been there to see it. You in the end my love, an awesome
dance indeed. Rama Mata sat in the front left of the room
together with her in-laws and close family members. My father
and I sat in the back. A big man owning the title of Swami began
a speech in a foreign tongue; the words thrown moved people
into tears and laughter. I wondered until a tinge of fear crossed
my own face if anyone would mourn my death, if I would prefer
to be missed or forgotten by the living, to be written and saved,
or have even a poem of mine escape the lips of a young girl in a
thousand years. Silence triumphed. People stood to begin
walking round the altar clockwise, prostrating to the feet of their
salvation once in front. I followed suit as a mime might have
done because it would have been the same if I were someplace
else, yet in this the dance removed me from my reality and shook
me to a temporary limbo of contemporary thought. To what
length did this man go to become the object of idolatry, he was
pure sex, do not fear the void when your hand is in mine his
marble lips spoke. A prayer came and all started to chant. Once
more all the people went silent. Lost now in neutral thought I
went unaware until we started out of the building.

      Well-wishers packed together poured from the mandir

going their own ways around the property. Maha Deva spotted
my expressed displacement and approached me with a winking
eye. Now was the time to feast, so I went for the hall to grab a
seat at a table while there was still plenty of room. Atop a
wooden stool I sat looking down at my reflection in the stainless
steel table and sadly questioned if anyone knew who they were,
if any had simply resolved to be read like children books, or if
most had retreated long ago into a place of stoic captivity. I must
be no different than the rest says the simple logician of the
pragmatic mind. Such fluidity to be as the river, only to live
passing courageous rocks. Leaves of the Areca Palm get placed
before each setting. My father found a place beside me and the
room quickly filled with people's conversations in countless
languages. Over three hundred languages in a country one-ninth
the size of the United states. A young boy came around with a
bucket and spooned a bit of its contents onto each of our leaves.
After a good number of buckets went around each person had an
array of foods, from vegetable bryani to a sweet dish with the
consistency of oatmeal named payasam. Everyone was happy
motivated by death. As is custom we ate with our hands, a
tradition with great reasoning. One smells the food, admires its
beauty and enjoys its taste. Why would one not also touch and
feel the food. The simple act of eating could be so different. Why
had my own way of eating become the way it was? Funny,
eating with a big silver spoon in an air conditioned room in front
of a flat screen television. Eating, not eating for months, starving
from famine, starving yourself, punished by vanity.

We finished the meal and left our seats to give others
space. Outside I admired the property. My father came along and
we wandered into a garden beside the hall, we each picked a
mint leaf from a healthy bush and rubbed it in our hands to enjoy
the aroma. Rama Mata soon found us smelling our hands and
giggled. She called for us to return to the main room where we
had sipped chai earlier in the day. Our friends had not yet
finished eating and remained in the hall. Those red couches

rested below us and with our full stomachs, we lounged. The high sun made the room hot and exhaustion fell upon us, taking us to sleep. When we awoke Rama Mata was smiling nearby. Most of the people had gone home, our friends, well wishers, and the majority of the others. Only women of the ashram hurried to clean up the day's mess. "And how have you seen your day?" asked Mata G. My first day light in India and my father's return after many years. "I'm fascinated Mata G, I love it." She looked into my eyes: " Do you have anything to ask me Prem?" "Yes," I replied. I didn't know what, my name I supposed, but I figured that I should come up with something more. What a boring person I am not to have questions. She told me to meet her on the patio outside in a few minutes so that we might speak alone.

Like those hypothetical questions we are asked near the night fires. Who would you sit with if you could sit with anyone in the world? And what question would you have for them? What question would you ask the wise? There she was outside sitting on an aged metal chair in her orange cloth. It was a place open to a flowering courtyard and birdsong. The air was heavy with dusk coming dew. I sat cross-legged on the floor before her. Did I need a new name? A new name to follow an old name that was lost to me. She laughed with her well kept secretes and stated that it was not necessary to do so but that I should remove Kumar, which means boy, from the end. She said that I was old enough to be spoken of as a man. The symbolic ideas of manhood have always escaped me; its absence in western culture keeps us from understanding its numerous roles. My second question: "Should I become an actor?" A silly question, what will I do? I, I want this and that. Lending the body to another's shoes, if only we had a thousand feet, but don't we now? "We're all acting every day," she said. "And if you know about these games of the world, you like them, enjoy them, acting is a nice choice. Instead of acting as one or two or three or four things the rest of your life as we must all do, you may act on behalf of countless things so simply."

You see Brando pissed off a good few people when he said his job was easy, to be a man of truths, that little heaven gaze he had; where was he looking or was it all a joke? To be calm and sit in this role. I respect the actor. The masters, please offend us and make us cry, make us feel the dark of Auschwitz and the light of eden, but god damn it if you cannot, do not scroll around with your televised attributes acting as the actor. We would all be so lucky to feel. The show of the feeling. Much more was said on that porch but so much more was on my mind that I was truly missing. "I love you Prem," she said. "I love you too, Mata G, I do." I stumbled like it was something of worth I would coward to jettison. How interesting it is to hear that somebody loves you, no matter the egoistic reflexes. I hadn't heard it with such soft honesty without any strings. I thanked her and started back for inside with wetting eyes. My father was to speak with her next. We are all loved and alone. I waited basking in graceful states of mind with Thalia-like thoughts. Because nothing ever seemed real, it was more special that I was loved, even if it was from some part of me that I had yet to discover.

My father slowly walked from the porch. Silently we toured around the grounds with no care at all. Evening Arati was running close, candles lit and from loudspeakers came a classical Indian tune sung by a young women with an angel's high-pitched voice. Two Pujaris walked under the horse drawn chariot leading to the temple. Ceremonies in which one pays homage to the idea of Lord in the deity form by offering incense, prayers, flowers, and whatever else you may see as necessary for freeing your mind from the troubles of your momentary false realities. I stood nearby, in a way indifferent, but entranced by my fleeting perceptions. Afterward, as I looked to the sky, the moon was in its crescent form just below the closely aligned planets, Jupiter and Venus, a smiling face above me in the sky.

These dreams do not belong to you nor to an end or a beginning
But your dreams you shot belong with you once after you've
stopped spinning
So do not worry nor send away these dreams that you've
embellished
Send your dreams from out your pockets above these grounds
we've cherished
For these are the dreams of the daylight dreamer so these
dreams have never perished

Back at the hotel that night the city was as dark as when we had arrived. A young Algerian couple stopped us in the main hall. They were tall and wore nice clothes and had all sorts of cameras and books on Indian tourism, they went on about how we must see the Taj Mahal and other such things, they seemed fast and out of touch. Why were they here? What were they doing and who were they? I couldn't tell, god it made no difference but still I was left angry at the modern west. It was the contrast that got me. Still, I am no judge. From what angle did I assume myself to be as such? We left them before they could tell us more.

In the hotel room Devi Dass and I spoke dazedly of the day. He was back to see the anniversary of his Guru, but also felt he was there to give closure to his idea of fatherhood. He wished to influence me, he assumed that I was lost and only the east could remedy me found. All in the same way he was also there reflecting on his own life. This is what stole his mind, he wished to see the truth and disregard his trembling mind in the face of his financial and emotional turmoil, he had no life to call his own and less company to join him on his journey. It struck me deep to see such an old sadness still swimming in the deep end of a man chipping love so hard off his shoulders.

The day was fresh in our minds but we thought it best not to diminish our experience by recalling the happenings or conversations. It's never right to speak of things before they set. For the sake of calm rest for himself and me, my father recounted a story he had often told me when I was a young boy. A story of my father losing his cats when he was a child. A fierce blizzard came and the streets were empty. He knew fare well that his cats were outside, and the story was his adventure to find the cats, which in the end were justly found. They had been hiding in a drain hole cuddled up together. For hours the cats meowed for help, my father could hear them but the wind carried their meows across the streets so he could not find them. The only reason my father was able is because they never gave up and trusted their friend would come. Eventually he was directly above the meow and decided to dig down. Although I left off quiet minded after this story my sleep was littered with dreams; dreams of being thrown about in waves crashing onto beach and dreams of the empty foulness feeling that love gives you when it is broken.

No longer does it save me from the dark and timid floor
the closet filled with monsters nor the basements blackened
doors
So sit there in the open with a scored fistful of tears
If those monsters ever roar she simply scares them off with fears

Vishwa Shanti ashram turned back to its mint state the following morning. After a short breakfast served in the dining hall we were escorted to the main room of the house for a good sipping of chai. Rama Mata came around and decided at once that she would be sharing stories with us. All of us children sat with big eyes expecting freedom to flow from the words of this woman. One freedom came with the ancient parable about the criminal that held no belief in mental freedom but had found it within a few years. The scholar of the story that believed and studied being thoroughly had spent his entire life in search of the constant epiphany but had never found it. If you truly do not believe water to exist, then the moment you see it all of your doubts shall cease. If you claim to know what water will look like before you see it, it may pass you by as a cloud and the great doubting ego will prohibit your notice. Something of the lesson I had yet to acknowledge. I somehow knew I would, I had to, I wanted to go to the end, to find the end and to watch it, willingly.

What had I planned for India, Rama Mata asked, and how long I would be doing it? I didn't know. It was beyond me. From what I could surmise then through my carelessness, I desired nothing to come of it, but was beginning to see worthiness in attempting to achieve control of my persons future, finding satisfaction within myself. The motivation behind this seemed finite, control the world and the people upon it, my "I," mass-produced, acted and forgotten. She smiled at this as I spoke satirically. "That's a good idea, Prem. You come back here before you leave and we'll see what you've learned. You should, you're such a happy boy, Prem." She pinched my cheek and smiled. Good people never tell you what to do, they give you only the wit to do what must be done. Wondrously I sat infatuated with my over-intellectualized ideas that me, myself, and I had no understanding of. What an idiot.

A young man with tones of wealth entered the room and introduced himself as Yogi, Rama Mata's son in law. He looked out of place. He was a medical student hailing from the United States but collected a good understanding of the local systems, and he spoke a scratch of a few of the local languages. Since my father and I were to be traveling India for a while, he thought it good that we go with him to check out the town and see a bit of rural India. We thanked Rama Mata for the stories with some type of misconstrued eye contact presenting us with the idea that our wish was to be perceived as people who knew the subject. We left her. Yogi called on Maha Deva and the four of us jumped into an old four door Mitsubishi parked outside the house.

Dirt roads brought us into a small town after some kilometers. A few pharmacies occupied old building stalls, and there were some restaurants with open fronts to the street, fruit and vegetable vendors, and a couple haircut joints. Lots of happenings but most of the people were just hanging around. People knew how to hang out there and do a whole lot of nothing. They know the truth about it, I mused, there aren't too many places that people know how to do a whole lot of nothing and enjoy it. Most of us succumb to the fantastical projects in the midst of the mind; let us go get something someplace. We parked in the front of a shop with "Dhaba" written on the front. To the side was a tiny stall the size of a hot dog vendor you might see in the big city of New York. A bowl of water was on the cart, filled with green circular leaves, and beside it were a bunch of cans of all shapes and sizes. Yogi uttered something in Hindi to the man, who looked at us with a big grin. Yogi had told him we were from United States and that we had come to India specifically to try pan. The man quickly took out two leaves from the bowl and placed them on the table, slapping some lime rock powder paste onto both with a brush. He then proceeded to add cardamom, bitternut, Beadle nut, some ground clove and other spices. In the end there were two leaves with miniature piles of spices and powders on the top. Yogi then asked if we would like tobacco in our pan. My father declined the offer but I chose to accept. I smoked for a few years but I wasn't taking tobacco at the time, I had quit to impress my father but felt the urge to succumb in this instance.

This drying spry vendor wrapped each leaf into a tight package, pinning it shut with a whole clove. Yogi instructed us to chew but not to swallow its contents, similar to dipping tobacco in the west. My father and began. Sensation filled us. Our mouths quickly filled with a dark red liquid, we spat horribly, making a mess of ourselves, pan juice dripping from our chins. By now a crowd of people were watching us, giddy, curious of our virgin pan experience. My head rushed, a little impractical for the effect, as it does stain your mouth red for many hours and leaves you with a strange acrid taste on your tongue. What a fucking novelty. The gringo parade. Yogi laughed at us and with us. Maha Deva let us know his opinion as well by telling more people in the street what these whites were doing. With the sun down the grounds of the Ashram grew quiet and cold. All that was left of the festivities was a curious thought: create, use, waste, repeat. Devi Dass and I were to be heading to Chennei the following day. Our farewells to Rama Mata would be soon and were built up to a grand level of dire importance, spinning around.

On the patio, Rama Mata placed a mala in my hand for the practice of meditation and mantra, she gave me a few words to repeat. I forgot them for I never listened but would try and desperately remember them some months later in search for salvation. "Be free and listen to your heart and not your mind, Prem." She embraced me and said that she would see me again in no time at all. I hugged her and in her embrace felt an air of pride take me, as if from her I took strength in myself, so it was an experience quite free from her entirely and entirely of myself. I looked to her eyes afterwards in a way I purposed to produce understanding but was lost in my own youth. I would only cry a year later for that moment, true tears of a humbled soul, I am awed. As my father prostrated to the feet of his Guru tears easily flowed from his eyes, he loved her so. She loved him as well, but the tears he shed held the dress of a self pity. To be shook silent. It was to see the presence of truth and in that presence to see that we are the long lost friend, the vanished hour and the mutiny from love, all while the mangrove hovers above the ocean.

You have been lying on your back and through your teeth.
Yet you're dyeing out in black but fail to stain beneath you.
This trying clout does smack but hails me to believe you.
The arena of these lies, a game, now do as we do.

Morning came again as it does; my father woke me explaining that he bought two plane tickets to Chennai. I spent what time I had on a blue couch with a view of busy road. Up north, the Himalayas, all of their glory, and the Andes; these two castles the history of words have seemed to strangle. We would make it up there together but once he left I'd try to be with them myself. To be alone, hadn't I always felt alone? No matter the company I held, I was stagnant but was there movement in change? I was alone and with another. We left off for the next leg of journey.

We stepped off into Chennai for no reason. To see more places and things of imagined importance. The myth, we needed it, but it watered hatred within me for all those who choose not to look at life in the fucking eye. We made our way to the taxi stand where a handsome middle-aged man approached us. " I can fulfill any of your desires and have a fine cab for transportation." Of course we went with him, this man was alive. I wondered what drove this poor fucker to such mad joy. We drove off in an old Fiat. The cabbie recommended a hostel by the name of Jana, meaning "wisdom" in Sanskrit. An old three-story place painted royal blue. A big sign was out front: "On roof deck restaurant with live musics nightly." A scrawny kid captained the front desk and he didn't speak any English; he gave us a room real cheap, more simple than the last. Rubbing shoulders with the poor man. The fact that we were sleeping in these old rooms with three inch mattresses and no hot water made the place seem more real. I wanted to live like this more and more as the days went by. It all felt more like home with nothing to bind me, but it was as if I did not deserve it, and still it was novelty just as the monkey doing flips. So truly I am fake but no further than greed in monopoly.

The noise from the roof took me from a little nap. Quietly I left my station and started up the stairs leading to an open roof with tables all over and some plywood covering a couple of old crates. A sitarist sat on a cushion beside a tabla player. They kept playing as I walked past, taking a seat in the back corner of the room with a paper pad in my lap. Low bars enclosed the area. I looked out and listened. I wrote.

Parrots that a drunk man lost claim collections as the others be;
yet she strains to be as quiet as the others see.
Apologies to the eyes in the gaping mouth;
Over there; my squaw queen dies whaling truth.
No more natives in his head.
In this hour I deem myself a loser to the bounce, for I am still on
the up before the fall comes to douse and breath this fire that I
have bellowed with a young mans roar; copious waters.
Run more, run farther, I am yours.

Kanchipuram was the epitome of what I visualized when thinking of mystical India. A city only equaled in its years by those of Benares. It is only what was once was before, slowly becoming what it will never be again. We took that same Fiat as the day before, that man desperately waited outside the hostel for the night as to take us once more in the morning. Driving on and on through more and more India that all blended together. A vast landscape of temples and ashrams came upon us and the only differences after thousands of years seemed to be the cars, electric lights, plastic, and of course my father and me. We were to visit the Adi Shankara temple, there a lineage of teachers dating back before the moguls have kept their style the same. The study of pure Advaita, the search for what is and becoming just that. A temple wider then its height, one part marble and another part sandstone. The driver would return. We removed our shoes and made our way through the cold dark entrance into a grand hall. At the end of the room an altar lay upon a stage, a man sat center engrossed in the depths of a meditation. We made our way back though the room where it opened to an archway leading through corridors where we could hear the voices of children singing Sanskrit Slokas. Stories remembered by repetition, an ancient way of passing down information from generation to generation. The writer of histories decides history; here in song it is the same. The game of telephone; the massage of an undulating account of what has happened thus far.

I was taking in the air that smelled of wet stone and flowers when a Swami approached us curious of our presence. He showed us around. First he showed us to a room where an elephant sat resting with its body covered in elaborate designs drawn with sandalwood paste. The elephant was ordered to bless me, and it raised its trunk and placed it upon my forehead. I thanked the animal and walked down past the children. They all pointed at us and laughed hysterically, whispering to one another. They wore only loincloths and had shaved all but a small portion of their heads, they were training to be priests and belonged to the Brahman class. We were a novel to them and they were novel to us. Were they stuck? I wondered. The swami gathered us both and took us into a smaller room and left us to wait. My father and I stood in the room together alone, completely absorbed in our own phantasmagorical atmosphere. When the swami returned he had with him another man, the next in line to become Shakaracharia. The locals referred to him as Laser Swami. "How is your India?" he asked. "Very well, but I don't know really." We accompanied him into another room where he thought we might sit and converse over tea.

Locals maintained the fact that this man could read your thoughts and change your state of mind just by looking to your eyes, hence the name Laser Swami. In my arrogance I decided once we had been seated that I might stare at him and see what would come of it. He didn't seem to mind and smiled as I did, his gaze severe and his eyes strong with years of stillness. "What is America like?" he asked. "It is a busy place," my father replied. "People are very busy." The swami had his disciples bring out maps of the United States so we could show him where it snows

and where the best place to grow tulsi trees would be. He found
it tragic that I and my father lived so far away from each other.
"A puja will be held and you will go," he said. Then he left to
attend other matters. The senior swami of the Shankaracharia
lineage would be performing the ceremony.

Puja by definition is reverence, honor, adoration, or
worship. My father and I sat on the floor below the altar awaiting
the ceremony. Two men entered the room with a baby cow and
sat it in the center with a pile of the grass in front of it to keep it
occupied. Another two men entered the room with a baby
elephant different than the one that had blessed us earlier and sat
it down beside my father and I. The elephant kept looking at me
with his soft eyes as if smiling and saying "I love you." The cow
as you may know is a sacred animal for the Hindus. Religiously
none eat the cow, use of the cow is limited to milking and
worship. The elephant is a representation of Ganesha, a
mythological deity, the son of Shiva, among other things
responsible for the removal of life's obstacles. To have the head
removed, what a blessing.

I meditated with the Puja but absent of deliberation. I
still questioned the fact of my traveling just as the sycophants
but for years missed the self I longed to see. Three long oms
concluded the inner silence that ended just as fast as it had never
begun. They escorted the calf and elephant from the room. We
gave our thanks to the temple folk and made our way out into the
streets that moved slower now that my eyes were slightly less
shut. The hungry looking driver saw our expressions and
recommended we go to an abandoned ancient temple dating back
a few millenniums. We drove out of town and came to the
ancient foundation. My father and I toured the grounds and lost
ourselves in the old relics. This reality changed and the
unrecognizable world around me gave birth, my perception,
alone in thought, lost to dreams, Hallucinations of a better life I
wished to escape.

Listen to the frightened Rabbits as they run benign to fly.
It rips the love from off the subject where the movement comes to
die.
All this make-less movement mandates rogue insides.
But as float doubts all dilemma as we watch these trees fall time,
You are me with all my words and we are ever mine.

In the afternoon when our senses returned we toured the local university. A place funded, built, and supervised by the Shankaracharia foundation. It was a rundown place but morale was high. We were greeted by the headmaster and taken along the campus into a back room. A room of archives. Before us stood countless shelves containing ancient Sanskrit texts, scriptures, describing how to see that you are what is around you, beyond and before, in prose, parables, epics, or song. The room smelled of mold and coffee, and contrary to what one might have imagined, we were told we could touch and investigate them for ourselves. They oiled the ancient parchment weekly as to prevent rot. These invaluable texts were placed innocently upon metal shelves, as if to say, disintegrate if you wish, we shall treat you like equals and will not be bothered by your age.

We were to spend a day more in Kanchipuram, then head north, to Rishikesh, our great fantasy. The next day we spent shopping for some Indian garments in the local textile district. We picked up a few traditional shirts and pants. Poor children in the streets left me in a state of self-loathing. They clung to my ankles and screamed and cried. They followed us as far as they could, they wanted only happiness. I could do nothing and would not give money, rarely is there a positive effect when donating to children of the street. Still, I felt like a sad king, appreciating in a cold place that ignorant affluence is among the world's worst diseases.

   The Shitabi Express goes all the way from southern India, Chennai, to the north, to the foothills of the Himalayas. The station was the epicenter of business and travel for the local people. The walks of life, herdsman, sadhus, families, businessmen, Nepalese, Muslims, Jains, Hindus, Catholics, animals, and all sorts of foodstuffs being transported. The Indian railway company employs more people than any other corporation on earth. Our reserved ticket led us to the second to last car, with quarters inside that were separated from the rest by a sliding glass door, four beds to a room. Two bench beds below and two fold-downs above. My father and I were the only ones to the cabin. We took off and the city of Chennai went on by.

 The readable world is dead without the poet. "I want to let you know that you have nothing to regret, fortune is nothing more than the understanding of any given situation, there is always a bright side to this place. And honestly we have far too little time to joker about" I had no faith in these words at the time. I said then what I knew to be true, but felt another way. The true passive voice of reason. My father, he was happy with this. He is an internal man by nature. And here I write something I think he might have said if he had listened to his heart: "Just make sure to be happy and learn from me, always learn from everything and never start thinking you've learned enough, because if you do, at once you'll be faced with a test that you cannot pass." Lessons of humility.

   We fell asleep that evening to the sound of metal tracks clattering. Morning, we arose to a knock at the door. "Chai, chai, chai," calls a man offering chai for five rupees a cup. I opened the door. "Two," I said in the Hindi I had overheard. We sat up on the benches with our eyes swollen, smiling at each other sipping the tea. "Was Chile anything like this, Prem?" my father asked, obviously alluding to the grander nature of our yet short journey.

*

A warm afternoon and summer was just a month away. My friend David and I were driving. He and I spent a great deal of time together in high school. In fact, just some weeks before he had been pulled over by the police on this very same bridge. We had just committed a theft of some thousands of dollars in items and hocked them for a good amount of cocaine. A cop switched his sirens on while we were letting some friends out. The white dust was in my pocket when my friend Dave stepped out from the car, and just like a scene out of a high school flick, when the door opened a beer can fell to the pavement. Each person was then asked to get out from the car to be searched and checked. I, the last one waited patiently in my seat knowing the only thing between freedom and years in prison was my ass cheeks holding tightly to the bag. When my turn came round the cop simply looked to my eyes and said, "Sir, you can go, walk on home." That's all you need to hear, really, because after that I thought a lot about escaping the place I found colorless.

In a good paradox as all the rest, although I was raised in a highly conservative and wealthy community, I was done so by a mother who had no faith in its rules, who had no faith in the barking aristocrats and less faith in the public school systems paid for by high taxes. She was an advocate for the creativity and free love that emanates from children, and did not see problems solved by chucking money in their direction. To be raised against the grain that has been destroyed by scared men is a rare and fortunate experience, even if it was torturous. So back to that particular day from where the idea to leave came about, stopped at a traffic light in view of my childhood apartment. Dave and I were growing tired of what we had made of ourselves. We spoke adamantly on behalf of leaving but it was just a feeling and some words. We all do what we need to do unless we don't and what a terrible thing that would be.

With these ideas David and I decided to approach our parents with the notion of leaving, and since we happened to be blessed with highly liberal good-time parents, after speaking with them about the idea of changing scene, we collectively decided that it would be appropriate to go out of the country for our last year of high school. After research regarding oversees programs and countless meetings with the drab administrations of the public school system, my mother found two unique professors, an American and a native Chilean who were running a kayak school. They agreed to take us through a custom made program for the year. We were to be allotted all the necessary credits for graduation and were the first two students from our school allowed to do such a thing. I am too fortunate for having received these gifts, for being removed, for almost going over the edge, for almost losing all possibilities of abdicating my social role.

My father wished to know my view of experience, but he didn't know me, he never spared the time to know very much. I'm afraid he led a life of stress and our dynamic never seemed to allow our true selves to show within its confines. He could not tell happiness as more than a word. He cried detailing his interpretation of my life, when I was moving from school to school, going to a school for challenged kids in a class with children suffering from autism, Asperger's, manic depression. He was proud that he enrolled me in school in California illegally. Through these years of fighting to grow up along these lines I was drugged-out by the well dressed city docs, the allopathic westerns letting blood from the hurt arm not one hundred years ago. It was all anger. I grew up with my father angry at my mother. I lived with only her and estranged my own self from loose interpretations from the fleeting male figures. For this I felt alone.

So I went sour, but then he waited to hear my spawning morals and personal revolutions. I valued of the late, discovering the vibe of ahsados and vino, how to make friends who don't speak your language, and friends who do, how to let go and be free from worries, how to rob a car, to roll joints, chug beers, kiss, fuck, and the destruction of the judgmental mind. To read and expand our tiny fucking minds, to dance and sing in the front of all. How to white water kayak and how to even begin to see the mountains and the trees for what they really are and are not at all. To see what love means and to feel the special meaning of these words and the irrelevance of them all. Tattoos and parties, making love all night and so much drink and smoke for the sake of the moment. Caramel quotes from another life.

Wide awake at six a.m. in our car eating bananas and sipping tea, our new destination appeared before our eyes. The scenery changed and the land appeared to have a more diverse group of people. We had arrived in Delhi, the capital of India. Our last stop before Rishikesh. We knitted our way through the station crowds, to the taxi stands, found a seemingly good guy and left north for Rishikesh. A place I had no ideas of, I had not seen one picture. I knew only of its epicurean nature by word of mouth. A pink arch similar to the one of Washington Square Park sat across a road. Along it was written "Serve, love and give." It was the entrance to upper Rishikesh. Temples, ashrams, monkeys, cows, and sadhus wandering the streets, a place for those who listen to the heart. The whole town rose from the Ganga into the surrounding foot hills of Himaleh. We rested in a hostel we found perched on the side of a hill rolling to the river near the outskirts of town. My father went to bathe. I went for some air. I wandered out and admired the views of town.

A glow around the gathering dancing in the distance
The show confounded parting thats now approaching mischief
I go to see and see to know these people prayed to endless
The glow around the gathering has ended in an instant

I am unimportant; my mind was scared at the uncertainty of its eventuality, fear of the unknown, how the organized religion has come to fruition? I wondered. What came first: fear that the sun would not come back or adoration of the sun for being so kind? What's the difference? I was worried about getting back to the life I had left behind. But in truth I couldn't even see if I had a life behind to miss. I am life. I walked the grounds trying again to come up with a reason for why I traveled to this place. Pacing, I excused my negative thoughts with the fact that these weeks in India had been the longest time I'd spent alone with my father. He would be leaving soon. I was all in my head. We were heading up to Uterkashi; Himaleh eased away my forlorn thoughts of my future.

Down by a cafe by the River we sat. The owner of the place greeted us. His name was Pranab. He was a guy that moved to a slow beat. He opened the cafe when his kids grew up and left for Delhi so he could still look after the hungry with tasty company. He was one of those guys you see and wonder what kind of life they had to leave them off at such a place. If I could act like him I would, but it would be a lie. I wonder if it is a lie to act a certain way, to become one on one's own accord. Sanford Meisner had some fascinating ideas for acting, like a pseudo-transcendentalist of the field, the truth is in the actual demonstration of production not the product itself, so if we see how the fire is made it is no longer magic. Anyhow, in the cafe two Israelis sat producing sound, one with a guitar and the other a flute. They played on about Israeli pride, nationalism, provocative insecurities. Who were they? Maybe they too were suffering from only fear and longed for the place they so desired to leave. We're children: the whole of us. I slept hard that night with a full stomach, no dream intruded my ventures, it went by with a blink and I couldn't say where I went. Another day and more perceptions of my continuous series of judgments. I awoke at dawn to the ringing of prayer bells in town, incense covered the air.

Money has not captured me,
It has yet to pull it's fangs.
White wild has not raptured me,
but he doesn't rule a thing.
A waste without us free,
In this sad unending blaze.
Money has too captured me, in this mad unending maze.

Down the road a ways we walked the bazaar in search of slacks and foods. Rudraksha shops, the royal blue berry before it comes to the seed they sell off. Kashmir tapestry all around. Artisan jewelry stores, and a good silver-pipe cut ring found its way onto my finger. We got a bunch of things and started over to a cafe by the bridge for tea. We were there as I see it to entertain hollow discussions of the emoting mind. My father and I had no handle on ourselves.

Devi Dass placed one of those orange bottles for prescription medicine in the center of the table. Anti-depressants, psychotropic drugs candied for the public. They are fun, yes, but the base argument still stands: to what purpose should they serve in the lives of children and parenting? Who should hold responsibility, the child, the parent, or the drug? He wanted to be rid of them himself, and my own view was from a bias he knew well. He thought there was no reason a man could need anything atmospheric to aid his mind-state. "I'm going to throw them off the bridge," he said. I shook my head in accord. I wasn't aware that he was taking these drugs until he openly decided to jettison them. True, we were always apart, but he had spoken countless times on the negative aspects of prescribed drugs. It angered me that he would so openly tell me this now without even the slightest preface. Something about it made me laugh at the fact that only here was I looking at my parents as people just like myself. I figured he had only recently fallen against his words, but with all things considered I had been living in a dark room, as we all are if we do not attempt an escape.

I remembered then a scene at camp during one summer, many summer seasons ago. I had with me my prescribed lithium, a drug used to prevent episodes of mania, a heavy piece. In my state of self-loathing, I hiked off the property late in the night and buried those pills in the ground. It was from fear of being controlled, conquered. I took my time burying them with a certain satisfaction that I had won a fight against people who swore it right to become as they were. We left the cafe and headed for the bridge. We stood there in the center as cows passed and the monkeys watched on. People made their way about the bridge, the pills fell from the bottle and spread out dancing into the Ganga, and my ideas changed base and saw no more reason in saving face. A motion to conquer the ego. We spoke nothing of it and walked off to continue our way around the town. We would head north the following day.

Dirt roads cut into the cliff, below swept the Ganga. We went out early and hired a driver from the taxi stand downtown. He was a young worker and spoke few words of English. We said only Uterkashi for our journey to begin. Being near December the winter was rolling in; the days were cold and the nights were colder. Halfway into the trip we stopped in an arduous mountain town and were told with body language that we should grab some foodstuffs and relax a bit before the second leg of the journey.

We sipped some tea from an open stall in the chilling air. "You know I never meant for it to turn out the way it did," My father said. He held regrets and I received them as resentment, that he defined himself as a failure. "I know, don't worry, it's not over, and anyway there is no use in being bothered by it. I love you whatever happened or will happen and you feel the same, I know it," I replied. "Yeah, well I'm glad we're together. It's been a long journey and this is the chapter closing," he commented. "I'm glad, too. It's been such an interesting time. It is indeed a good ending to something."

My father always saw life as some sort of war, or maybe a strange novel. I saw it too but wondered if that would ever leave us. He always spoke of monetary problems but always had nice things and houses, a second wife, a journey marked with sacrifice as he saw it. To be rash and arrogant as well, people make their own problems, so often we choose to blame trifles on things like money or women. It is only lack of love, the selfish love that is missed by many and spoken ill of if misinterpreted, the true love of self. Somewhere there on the lines growing up I saw we may never love another if we do not first love and know ourselves to the uppermost degree. And as an arrogant thought passes, metaphor. The one that must love first is the one that's loved. Emerson's acorn lives within us, water the folds and know them to be true.

The old town of Uterkashi was recently destroyed by an earthquake and landslide. With our driver unable to inform us where the place we sought was located, we decided on a hostel for the evening, one built into the far hill of the market. The man at the desk was a rugged guy. "Tourist season is over," he laughed and said. "It's cold, too cold for us, too cold for you." We didn't care, we were there for reasons that couldn't be excused by merely weather. He gave us a room on the second floor.

I started back for the lobby to order some chai for the moment and dinner for later. I walked back down and found the man who had given us the room; he was sitting on a couch watching an Indian movie with two friends. They were engrossed by the film so I knelt before them and asked if he could ready us some dinner for later and prepare two chai beforehand. The three of them laughed. "Doh chia my friend, and doh talie no problems," he said. "Thank you," I replied in the

Hindi I picked up from Namadeva.He bowed his head."Where are you from?" he asked "I am from the United States." "America, no?" Embarrassed. "Yes, America," I answered"You know Amitabh Bachchan, yes?" he inquired."I do not," I stated.He stared wide eyed. "He is Clint Eastwood of India, so much famous! You must see him now!" The tube television they were watching played an old film of Amita Bajans, *Zanjeer*. I sat and watched. Two steaming chai were placed in front of me. The three friendly guys looked me in the eyes."Enjoy, young American." One of them started to sing David Bowie's *Young American*. Another one of them slapped the singer in the back of the head, and they all laughed. We laughed ourselves to sleep that night, partly from the spice in the meal and partly because of the cold weather for which we were so ill prepared. As sunrise went we walked around the town. An old scooter half covered in soil was left over from the landslide. The whole town looked sad from being sick and dreary from the absence of business. A man in a stall fried up some parathas. We sat down and ordered a few.

 Two elderly men seated on the banks of the river wrapped in blankets smiled at me with their oceans of faces as I walked on by. They were sitting and watching it all go down, I was truly jealous of the station they so calmly occupied till death it would seem. Himaleh, to be drastically overcharged for silly literati; wombs of patcha mama. Soon we came to an old sign posted to a gate with a painting of Keshvadas. Mandir was written below. A rough man who looked after the plants told us the woman in charge had left just a week before and wouldn't be returning until the next season. A young student Pujari was left to take care of the place. An American man stayed there as well in one of the houses built on the land. He had been living an aesthetic life for many years, he was hermit. This made me question how far one can go alone. His eyes seemed lost and his step loose.

Two blue temples with pointed roofs stood and faced the

Ganga. Singing, talking, walking, thinking, mysterious entities ending up in this place, this place, it smelled as something I knew from another time, something like the first winter airs on the east coast. Only birds and water were heard. No rooms were available on the temple grounds, a room beside the temple land would suffice. My father went looking for the owner. I stayed behind and admired the natural flowing fountains and flowering flowers, and still even with all this I was internally restless. I placed my bag on the ground and wandered over to the river's edge. I used both my hands to take a drink of its water, delicious. *Why have I not grown up in this place? What drives people to live so tightly knit? Is it all fear?* I had no idea, but if heaven was on earth then why would one not live in it and reap copious amounts of mental freedom and love? A state of mind maybe? Just try and find nature in the Ford Taurus, you can if you try hard enough, maybe others see it with no effort. A useless thought.

Sunset came and the pujai rang a bell that hung low in the temple. Devi Dass and I started down for the entrance and removed our shoes. We sat upon the chilled white marble floor. The pujari chanted Lakshmi Narayana mantras, ideas of wealth. I sat in lotus posture drifting off into a deep silence. The air was of sandalwood and lavender. I was troubled with stilling the mind. I could not escape my desire to know my fate and conceptualize all possibilities of my so far bland journey. I wanted money. I wished a war upon us, an exiting explosion of any kind. I was not amused enough. More motion, less thought, anarchy. When it comes we see it and try to paint it just as fast but when we realize the paint has all run dry and the canvas set fire we cry at the war for limiting us, a sideways frown. When silence came I sat in emotionless of which I knew very little, all within and all without. Some good spots of time as Wordsworth would have said, if I understand him right, but still I was restless, still I wanted an easy woman and a fistful of green money. There was an element there that made it clear I wanted a death. On the third night I wandered out from the room for a bottle of prescription cough medicine I knew to be available. I drank the bottle to numb the senses, for they were too much for me, I had gone mad with all sensual terminologies and pointless words and laws, roles, god damn lines, my first BWM I drove around wasted and high on cocaine, booze, bud, and wine with a woman beside me. All went slow but the eternal seemed to only further facilitate hatred in an ego of bullshit. Again to murder the concept of ego, the word comes to the page. A better word, pez.

The next few days were dreary and sick of memory. I spent good times in some sort of an amorous meditation looking for home, and I wanted a death more when I could not find it. And while we ate our meals by an outdoor fire beside the clear river I wanted to death there, too, for I could not even see the fire as I knew it was. The electricity was off and the sun went down early over the mountains, nothing more than this, no place else to go, find me death, I call stalemate. I was internally cold and wished for silence, a home in which I could feel safe and free from strife, and this was it, and it overwhelmed to see the heaven of which I had not even enquired.

Basho never lonely out within that nature
Basho blooming harvest reaped for poems we cannot pay for.
Basho danced as all the rest and always
Basho brimming smiles upward setting free these foreplays.

The pujari told stories of his family but I do not remember them, I wanted only for my life to end. Him and the other guy working there wanted to go to America. They were better off in India but they persisted, insisting serendipity had left them behind along with all the other mountain peoples. The greener grass always escapes us.

These were simple days we spent there. My father and I got close without speaking of the useless things. We spoke very little of anything. I tried one last time throwing myself into an absurd place to find faith or satisfaction or hope or something of this nature, the feeling that the animal always dreams of after leaving the void of some other sort and so be it. She spoke nothing and afterward I crouched down by the river and spoke to my emotion in the personal tongue. I did not know who it was, and spoke only to a stranger. No closer there, only a skipping, simple. Nothing came of it. When in the end we bade our new friends farewell the Pujari gave us a ride to a taxi stand in town on his scooter. I had missed the place before I left, but had left before I had even arrived.

The ride back is always shorter. With curiosity dead we no longer pay attention to time and figure reflection is better left to its place. We drove fast on the cliff side roads weaving in and out of traffic, fresh dew was in the valleys and the newly damned up reservoirs made out little clouds that moved fast closely to the land. Rishikesh appeared after dark with its lights showing in the night, my preconceived salvation. Topovan is the upper town beside the river, Lakshmanjula is below, its bridge crossing the river. Devi Daas was wandering around and had come across the main gates leading into an ashram looked over by a woman by the name of Vanamali. A lanky boy guarded the property. He approached my father and told him that she was to be out for the next few days. We knew long before that she lived in Rishikesh but we had not made any formal plans. I met her when I was a young boy in northern California while attending a theater camp for children. She was giving talks on the meaning of love and the interconnected universe.

There I had come so far, so far across the world to see a familiar face, to be reacquainted with adolescent interpretations of manifest love. My father so wished for me to reunite with her. He saw it as the goal of his trip. Indeed, I had spoken adamantly on her behalf for many years after the first time I met her, but then I cared for her as much as I cared for the sky and the street.

Who was I to not satisfy myself first before all things. My father
took that I had been deeply moved by our encounter. It was from
the others who had made up their mind and I merely followed
suit as we do, still it is organic and real as the next thing. Before
my cumbersome demand for individuality was temporarily lost
to a race, a part of me imagined her to be my earth angel.

Dancin' cross the valleys on these open neon fronts,
where chance is lost to allies and to the kids who wear the
dunce.
She implies that it is all fine then that you do not mind the rain.
The smoking neon sloths lay lounging out without their names.

      And now came Christmas eve. The air was listening and
dry. My father was due to leave. Vanamali was walking the
grounds of the ashram when we arrived, and she greeted us by
the gate. As always, she wore a bright purple shawl with the
color and vibrancy of Hebe flowering in a late summer. She had
bright brown eyes and her smile was inviting. She told us we
must come in, sit down, have a chai, and speak with her and her
brother Mohan. They both recognized me from eight years
before. Of life Vanamali insisted without insisting that we come
to understand the values of inner silence, of love. That it be
selfless and of earth, it be clear that we be upon it without
assumption or colors drawn from the fear of others. Mohan
spoke of his journeys, he was the disciple, his journeys were
Vanamali. They were both as simple children under the skyscape
lingering above us. With them I dreamed that my journey was of
the kind that would end with me in a place of satisfaction,
happily ever after without a thought of difference and that when
death found me or be it so that I find death, I might do so a
happy man with worn shoes with dirt from a happy place. Her
purple wished me to see more of life. The existence of such as it
were lugubrious thoughts of the life as piece and parcel, too my
belief to where rests all the other things, because there cannot be

another color after we have grabbed the first three. We made a date to return the next day, which was Christmas.

As the gift my father presented me with a small brass murti of Ganesh. I missed the interest in the celebration and had nothing to give him in return. Sullied by the sport of life, I felt empty in spite of the idea of holiday. The groundskeeper opened the wrought-iron gates and waved for us to enter. The purple gardens of lavender, lilac, and meadow rue took my sad away. It was a purple and green place. He led us to the lawn behind the house where Vanamali and Mohan sat comfortably on wicker stools sipping tea. The Ganga flowed below. Out from the house came an elderly women. She was of the lowest class set for a life of labor, and it was only her that removed me from Neverland. What the fuck did it mean that this women took this role and that others supported it? Was it to take, to be given or pushed upon the one receiving this nasty gift? Karma, they say, merry Christmas. Was it really that simple that I can even talk about it?

A veritable feast was served, fresh chai, naan, papadam, and dishes from the south. Mohan and Vanamali were originally from Kerala, the most southern tip of India. "What do you think about the use of Chai?" asked Mohan after lightly taking a sip from his cup and returning it gently to the table. "Just tea you mean, the use of tea?" I responded. "Yes, of tea, Chai, what do you think about its use. Most cultures have tea. Here now we drink tea." "I could not say. I have never spent much time with tea culture, a lubrication maybe, maybe it is an excuse to speak to others on a more relaxed level because one may enjoy tea while conversing." "Maybe, but this is its use." He lifted his cup and took a sip, then looked out over the Ganga and all the hills and then smiled at Vanamali. I could see what they were after in their eyes,

I tried only my best to synthesize the bliss they looked to own. A Langur monkey ran onto the lawn to steal a flower.

Christmas. We thanked Vanamali for making us feel of home.
Home, the feeling, the feeling felt anywhere, past the irrelevance
of place and people, what is home, Lynyrd Skynyrd's home,
Edward Sharp's home, Jethro Tull's home, Steely Dan's
home, Etta James' and Otis Redding's home, Ozzy Osbourne's
home, Carl Sandburg's home, Robert Frost's home, Emily
Dickinson's home, Wang Wei's home, Walt Whitman's home,
we are home and I know to be home but so wish to be home,
why can I not see that I have been hoaxed to roam in my own
house scared by the girls and boys my own parents have gifted
me. Opinions of pain.

      The Raga is brought alive by the sitar and tabla. Raga in
Sanskrit translates to mood or color, the type of raga can specify
times of year and types of day the music can most pleasantly be
heard. A magnificent looking elderly Indian man dressed in a
grey kurta sat onstage next to a younger, smiley, potbellied man
dressed in a white dhoti with no shirt. Across the lap of the elder
sat a sitar, in front of the younger two shiny drums. We had
wandered into a cafe beside the Ganga, a sign outside read "Live
musics." Curiosity came at a swell time; as we walked in the
concert began. Only a small gaggle of whites sat in the audience.
A speech commenced the concert, the idea of ragas changing
one's state of mind, projecting one's thoughts to a plain of an
abstract nature. I sat with my father and the others. The players
spoke about music as an expression of love. There in a dark
room draped in multi-colored tapestries smoky with incense and
a bit of hash. Indeed this is how the pivotal moments of epiphany
should begin. Sitar played solo for what seemed to be a long
while, the Tabla came in at a moment of crescendo. I stay too
infatuated with myself. I only want to be held, I yearn to return
but fear lies in the heart that is soiled by the fierce blows of
youth. I left the world and went for a swim in the place without
words and histories. They left center stage as they had come on;
smooth, silent and selfless. I sat on the floor of the restaurant
sipping tea. A new energy was about me, my father as well,

sleep would come easy this evening; good night my friend.

Overlooking the Ganga my father and I sat eating breakfast at the devraj cafe. I sipped a tea enjoying the air. A man from beside me leaned over. "What are you doing here in Rishikesh?" he asked. He was a western Swami and his name was Bhodi, an absurdly confused philosopher of a man I would come to love and hate as the seasons. I told him plainly that I was there simply to have a good time. He laughed at this, and looked unsatisfied with my answer. It was just that, I was there to have a good time, he was here to blast out his persona of the professor. My nonchalance was equally misunderstood by myself as it was by him, but maybe I felt that way then, I cannot know for sure, even a lie would be of no use. A soft spoken German was in his company. "If you are here just to have a good time, then come with us for a meditation."
My father scolded me. "You're not here just to have a good time. Tell him why you're here," he whispered. I was here for this yet my father wanted me to say that I was on a spiritual journey to find my true self or something in this line of bullshitting. It was all bullshit in the title and I refused to go along with saying these things. I am here, where are you? Facebook? You mad millionaires, you children with keys to the gun shed, run, keep running.

My father and I were given an area to meet Bhodi later. The evening came and as we made our way over to the place he had told us to meet him, a car horn sounded from behind. A retired ambulance from the eighties pulled up beside us and a sliding door opened. Bhodi and his German friend were inside, they both looked excited. We piled in and started off on paved roads towards the north that soon turned into unkempt dirt roads. We drove on for a good while until we came to a corner where we could see the beginning of another valley, we pulled off to the side and were motioned to get out and look around.

"Look over there where the green crop begins. I'm gonna buy a piece of land a little ways further than that. I want to make an ashram there for people from all the world to come and meditate without having to live in the cliché of Rishikesh," Bhodi said. A good man, I thought. I saw reason in that statement, as I was a stubborn realist as well, I suppose. It was all getting quite psychiatric, wasn't it? But do not fear, it was only the beginning.

We drove farther on and soon arrived above an old ashram on the banks of the Ganga. The place was built around a cave titled Vishishta Gufa. *Gufa* translates to *cave* from Sanskrit, Vishishta was a saint who had sat inside that cave to achieve a state some call enlightenment or the great sounding, sitori. He passed away many years ago, only his disciples remained. Men lost on a lifelong journey to realize life. We parked off the road and made our way down long winding stairs. All the residents were silent as we passed on through. At the far corner of the land that lay on the banks a sheer wall went up towards the hills. Right against it stood a wooden door that led into the cave. The four of us silently entered the dark tunnel lit by a single candle. We followed it back to a room nearly the size of a van, sat down, and began to meditate in its somber darkness. The cave seemed to undulate with vibrations and deep sounds of the churning earth. I felt the smooth stone ground beneath my body. Timely rooting and some auditory hallucinations. I sat and began to feel my breath and be rid of the thoughts that scathed my everyday. Here now some moments of silence, moments that catch us off guard, and visions teeming with my own religious allegory.

I was the first to leave. I left quickly because I was intimidated by these revelations of being and when I came upon the light of the outdoors I was moved anew by the landscape around me. I was more alive and could feel the life in my fingers. I wandered over to the banks of the river and sat atop a boulder. I looked at nothing at all and everything at once. The

German girl was next to exit. She wandered by the place I sat and found a spot in the sand. As she passed we did not speak, we exchanged only heavy smiles and stoned eyes. My father and Bhodi came out from the cave, and they too sat on the banks. After some moments I wandered over towards the water. I sat in the sand gazing at the trees across the way. Bhodi came and kneeled at my side.

I began to utter some word for thought but the moment I let out a sound, Bhodi held up his right hand and silenced me with a small wave. "If you wish not to listen to the following words it is of no consequence, but if you desired to hear them well, it would be a useful term." He went on: "If we did not speak unless we truly believe the words, feel them, and know them to be true from within the heart, for words alone are only sounds. This world would be a better life."

I took in the advice, for I never did wish speak unless I felt this way about the contents of which I was sharing, yet had always done the back side, sweet speech, a good hassel. Because words lost to the masses are the words that no one hears, and words wasted are the ones spewed in honor of nothing but the speaker himself. My mind trembled in the face of this paradox, really something, which all ideas suffer from, this fact that all things have another side due to the popularly perceived apparent dualistic natures of reality intrigues my treasury yet denies me cautious entrance . To me, on numerous conclusions; nothing was worth speaking of, only the epiphany, which, when vocalized, is lost anyhow. We made our way back past the ashram and up the stairs one-by-one. We drove home in silence, and bid farewell with few words. Dropped off in town near our room my father and I made our way to the nearest cafe for our last tea and conversation before his departure.

The cold morning to which we awoke well before the sun chilled the eyes. It was dark and no one was about; he had tried to see that he and I could see some meaning together, and so I could fall in love with something and stay behind and journey towards it on my own. In the street that lined the Ganga I packed my father's bags into the back of a white cab, one of those old ones. Sadhus slept on the stairs leading back to the ashram. My father's tears came as he hugged me goodbye. I didn't cry for I was being the man of rare emotion and wanted him to know that I was something of a man. I was alone now with a deepening sense, I hoped he knew the same feelings as I. He whispered in my ear, "You'll be fine alone won't you?" "I'll be fine. You don't have to worry about that. You stay fine yourself old man."

We laughed, and again my father's eyes wetted. " I will. You know this time we've spent together has been worth all the trouble. I hope you find what we are all looking for. I love you."" I love you, too." It was said with a smile as my gaze cast up towards the sky. "Our time has changed a whole lot of things, with us, with me. Don't worry."I stood in the road as the cab pulled away, I watched as is went. Warmth took me and I knew I was safe and still awake. If there were no other clouds beside that one up in the sky, with its shadow drooping down, I saw it well. One floated fast above me.

Through these seasoned suns it will rain to the ends that will come.
As we arise from the plain, we shall sit here and hum;
Back man, back man, such kisses for the pain.
It has all been a thought.
Be rid of your Mane.

Rishikesh

Chapter Two

An odd, thin brick building rested on the land of V above the Ganga. This is where I was to stay: a square space on the second story with a cot and a wooden desk beside the barred window. A washroom was off the patio and from there, a few stairs led down into the garden of purple across from the main house. My view above the entrance gate looked out over the busy streets. I stayed here and it was a pleasant place but it was not my intention to stay long. It was as if as if it was a chance to look upon the world from the eyes of books and hearts of strangers. I wished only to be a part.

He was Thorazined and brought unto this empire, balanced to turning whilst spinning last mirrored. While you were out an economy collapsed, fuck him if he knows. There they are getting high in the bush. Brothers of evil and of the doers for good, predecessors of the slaves, blinding beams. Cowboy dancing, money hungry, black gold on top of blood. They play of war for fun. Lots he doesn't know, breaking all the rules. All these country lines flabbergast this mind of mellow drool. Sold and grey, scared running high. Honor left the building with the man who fights to die.

With a little day I pressed flowers with a vice then let them set. Vanamali sold them on handmade greeting cards for

money. The children ads close singing for the temple. Rock
formations enclosing manmade imaginations. One boy would
often approach a statue of Krishna with a bland morose face, he
would look around him as to see that no one was his audience,
and if no one was seen he would smile and begin a jovial
dialogue with the idol. Above this room in which I watched and
worked, Arati was performed. I would frequent the ceremony
and imagine each time to be more silent and less affected by
moments without. I did little other than these simple things.
Vanamali had made it clear that I should do much on my own
and as much as I wished to make myself content. It was little I
wanted and even less I said as the days went on. The times I
devoted to the sitting I figured to be relevant, I would be there
until the mind goes playing tricks. I laughed as all the other
things followed suit and joined him triumphant in the center. If
there were other things to be considered in all of this I do not
know, but when satisfied with these fictitious trifles my eyes
opened to a view of the Ganga that meant for me a certain clarity
still ran through the world. Even if it was just through the myriad
movements of my Rishikesh.

Ain't no flags on my moon nor no names in that sun.
Jamess vagabond Jr.. John candy Jr.

Sleep was gone for the find on the land of V. *I, a*
contemporary, what shall I do? Standing for youth I must
attempt to know myself, but must I already? It has all been done
before, and here I am thinking beyond what I am now, what I
wish to be? But had I been thinking all along to stop and think
about these thoughts then where would I be then, or now?
reflections of the reflected. I had no explanations of my inner
rant, but another part of me thought of hubris, then came a
memory of a man named queen who spoke to me on the idea that
life would be deaf and dumb if we're without symbolism. I argue
it to be a torture to live among expectation; this symbolism; mere
interpretations of the individual perception. A traveler spinning

in his own perceived omens that may only double back upon themselves each step they make as we have just here, it is all the same. To be sheltered from the storm that never shows; an interloping mind that smiles only when the end approaches, or perhaps shudders in fear. You know, I knew I hadn't wasted time, I had no such things to waste, for then I knew for certain that progression did not live there, only thoughts. Thoughts that went a mess and fell upon the next electric round.

You see how I could not sleep? I removed the blankets from my warmed body and slipped on it some cotton. I left the room and started down for the Ganga. The streets, open for store owners and sadhus and whomsoever wished to sleep there gave an empty feeling that resembled an envy of those who called the street their home. Slowly I made my way, cows stirring and then a rouge monkey briskly skipping before me. The sound of wind came and went and it smelled of garbage on fire. The cement in the center market, full of silver plastics, an herb shop barricade owned the symbol of universal vibration written beside an opposite going swastika, a samskrtam. As we become more empty, everything speaks with us; everything frowned as I looked round with an air of debonairness. I got to the banks and sat watching the water wave by down south with a certain sense of shame. I am the rich, spoiled, white, the Malibu aphorism. How dare I relate to the epics of contemplation, as if I were to be in this place to simply to learn what others hadn't the time for. A contrived *Eat, Pray, Love* cliché. I was jealous of the suffering but at the same time defied the call of suffering, calling it out for the dead noise that it was, emanating from the poor quarters of the heart. The hum of a fox came from a close. Such a fool to be wasting brightness; to be taken aback by my own foolish censorship. I was scared to move forward with what I knew, but what I knew was not nearly enough to satisfy my need to know more. I wanted to know everything all at once, but knew that there was nothing more to know at all. The heart knotted with the paradox of satisfaction absent of the courage and steadfast of youth. Time passed, and as it does for us all the sand ran through my fingers and the moon escaped the silver stream. I was returned. Oscar Wilde laughed in my direction. The sun began to come out from behind the mountains and as it crawled I sauntered back to my room like a wild patient and slept 'till it rose high once again.

My nights went like this, only small inconspicuous things changed. I argued alone and fought over nothing considerable. Sleeping soundly became more and more rare, unwanted dreams of things I might have done invaded my nights. A naked man stripped down to the bone shuddered sobbing in a dark corner while chained by the ankle to a diamond larger than he. The matador's bingo for death accomplished for pride. This one; this young blue-eyed rubio spoke from further and further a distance as each day became. I suppose I might have continued eating meat and drinking alcohol along with all the other things just as I might have continued thinking from the same place, and havent we?. But Rishikesh is not only a dry town, absent of booze, but vegetarian as well: by law. The more that is taken away, the more I shall be able to feel, to feel more fully than before, and what do these things matter anyhow?

I left myself again with nothing left to win. My chips out do my woven pockets right up to the brim. Fuck it all to this blue breeze wind. My canary diamond ring still rings, and although the darkened shaft lights begin to linger, still canary sings.

To keep my mind off things, or rather on track as not to become lost, I had Vanamali, and although she knew little of my internal dramatics she was a saintly woman. Each day I was with her I felt more confident that I could reach perfect happiness. She would write and eat, sit and softly speak and sing. She would work on one of her new books she authored on the psychological forms of mythological gods. Mohan was also there and would remind me often that few men can still be as pure as we have imagined them to be when we were children. He was a learned man, a scholar of medicine, yoga in all its forms, and eastern philosophy. We see a new society fresh from the turbulent trifles of creations, cultivated from the dreams of the traveled and of the put, of the confounded and equally as wise, Darwin running round with this here blind impetus. The useless labels and justifications destroy ideals just as far as the societies that have created them in their own demand for the greener grass, as I have done. Break never free from patterns of contentment, we be as brother and sister in love without colors; good people.

I wish from out my well
To end this space of sinking spell
In kissing you I trust that you'll grow twirling near my side
But in missing you I must not know the seek from out the hide

Opposed to my thoughts and inquisitions, my mental motions, I mention now a female monk, a good woman that showed me to a good piece of my mind without knowing me at all. I saw her very little and left the town in such a hurry I never thought to knot my ropes. It was like this in all the places I went and with all the people I met: in, out, and gone without a thought of difference. She was the daughter of a western man who came to live in Rishikesh way back when. She was doing the whole of this and that and had a way to her; she was most coarse but so sweet a woman I shan't compare her to another. Beyond this chore of which she took willingly, she seemed as if she had walked the wrong path but knew far too little time was left to turn back, a sad idle life. Only others felt free from the creations of her malice. She spent her time maintaining a clean Rishikesh, a noble cause where the meaning of trash has gone missing. Trash had always been something that would go back to mother earth the same way it had come, the ground. Now with the use of plastics this case is fairly strewn due to the forty-thousand year degradation period of said plastics. I have been witness to only a handful of winters.

Trash was everyplace but did not look like trash here, never was there room. Recycling signs led me to a homely looking business situated up the hill a ways from Jara road. A few rundown buildings sat on a land with fenced in areas designated for different groups of garbage. Five guys sat around a fire, the elder of the bunch came out and stepped to my front. "I am Dinar, and you see all this, this place is what I do, you are welcome." He was direct like that. Dinar was the manager and if one can look as such, Dinar looked as if he held the utmost devotion towards his work and felt spiritually obliged to do so. He made this known to me by the way he nimbly walked and the way he stared directly into space as if his eyes had already found a place to rest. He smelled of spice and gasoline.

A boy and I climbed a eucalyptus near the fire, at its height I watched the hills going into the Ganga. "Very simple life here, out of mind, out of body," the boy stated in Hinglish. "Yes," I laughed, "an easy place to get lost." "Yes that is possible, anywhere it is possible, but maybe it's too good here and people lose track of why they have come," he said. A good many white stragglers roamed northern India, these dogs never returned. Perhaps they never found the *it* of which they sought and in the name of their king dwelled in question forever? We descended, found some gloves with the rest of the men, and made our way down the hill to an old makeshift pickup. The boys and I piled in. Dinar drove. I and the others stood in the back bed. Along the streets we laughed, my Hindi was atrocious and we mocked each others' attempts to communicate with hand signals and facial expressions. The truck stopped close by Laksmajhula, the upper town right close from where we had come. High day, all the people are in the streets: incense vendors, people looking for work, people working, and tourists from south India. Children running, packs of dogs rummaging through garbage, a big white cow I had often seen in this very place was eating a pile of spoiled lettuce and the mischievous monkeys were perched on the rooftops spying on the life below. Dinar took me to walk with him, he was going to be collecting the monthly payment from the shops who practiced recycling. All the proceeds went straight back into the project. We went off as the other boys separated to clean up the streets by hand.

This blinded blinding waster white man- I throw around my plastic junk
My colored waters, shiny wrapped cookies and money for lunch
Yet the conscious is unharmed because it is not me,
the world must clean itself you see, I the ignoramus
Go find another remedy awful bastards, your late for the party,
the consumers, deniers, the pickers and flyers
Staunch laughter and fat bellied greed, you've taken more than you'd ever need, and then you took that last fruit moments before the seed.
Now we are finished. Speed.

On the rounds we walked the town slowly. It was until we encountered a character man that I was unconscious, he referred to himself as Babu. Babu owned a jewelry store on the other side of the river across the bridge. When we entered his shop, he invited Dinar and me into the back room for some tea and words. I sat down in an old leather chair, Dinar sat in one similar beside me. Babu sat behind a dark wooden desk and called a young man over from the store front and ordered his service."Do you know the reason you are here?" Bubu asked, holding his belly." Hell I do, I've got to know something, right?" I replied." And what is it?" Myself and Dinar are here to receive your monthly payment for recycling," I answered confidently.
"Partly correct. There are more reasons, yes?""Quite possibly, Babu," I said, pondering foreseen bulls shitting. Everyone wants to be the fucking Guru, I thought. Dinar smiled as the servant returned, three steaming chai found the table. The room smelled of honey and old playing cards. "It is quite possible now is it not

that you are here because of fate, that fate has brought us together, that you are here to learn something from me and I am here to learn something from you, would you agree?""Sure I would, Babu." I agreed to play."Then you must tell me something of intrinsic value.""I'll make an attempt, but I doubt it'll succeed in tickling your fancy.""This is possible then?""Yes." "Then I am ready." I sat for a moment, and remembered some different pieces of text."In the Peruvian Amazon there are a variety people, I now speak namely of shamans. They and others have been ingesting organic concoctions or entheogenes for thousands of years, Babu, and some say they can read plants on a molecular level as to further understand their use and nature. I mention my obvious fascination because it removes communication from contemporary language and relates it to vibrations and other such ethereal things that function alongside natural emotions, moods, and other things that cannot be so easily misinterpreted as spineless words. But Babu, this is a waste of time." What a waste of time. Would you like to know a little about a lot or a lot about a little? "I know it, and you know it, it's pointless information so we can further compartmentalize our terrified mind, like that there is enough DNA in our bodies to go to the sun and back 610.9 times, Van Gogh's "Starry Night" was painted on my birthday a century ago, the original synthesizer of LSD passed away at an age well over ninety and he was physiologically reasonable, by this I mean his mind was fine, our last president was a cocked out spoiled rich kid, our current presidents wife made around five hundred thousand dollars at her last job and she was working at a hospital in Chicago, a hospital, Babu, a place designed to help people, save people, or to help them give others money in a long bureaucratic nonsensical way, to save them so they may pay another day, but what a shame. Imagine if I knew the terms and regulations of something corporate, Babu. Wouldn't that shake you up so?"

Babu looked at me with squinted eyes, I don't think this

is what he wanted, sarcastic jabs from a depressed outlook on transcendentalism. He laughed still."This is all very nice but what does it have to do with the self?" This was almost spoken like the monk at the environmental summit."Nothing, Babu, nothing. Nothing does. It's a shit storm. We love people but know they are to shut in to be connected. It's like the great dictator speech, Babu, in our hearts of humanity we all love people but are scared that no love will come in return. We are not who we want to be, rather, who we are wanting to be which we are now is not the person we are, but isn't it?" We laughed, but it seemed I was coming from a dark place. "Babu, I really have nothing to tell you. Maybe I'll come back in a few years when something useful comes to mind."The tea, and I forget the tea on the table."This was interesting, your mind is of value, or of little or no value, but honesty is the epitome of love. As for me I have little to tell as well that would be of use, only, be among the crowds as you would be alone in a cave." Even softer words followed, but we had to be going, there was more work to be done and more things to be said. Still I do not remember the taste of that tea.

Forget about those dust covered items atop the top shelf.
Forget about me friend your no further of use to even yourself.
Your the top cruise tommy gun thats gone and shot itself.

All along a part of me was curious to learn postures of yoga. Eventually it became justified just as my breath and then recessed again to a place of lesser importance. At this time I speak of, a large side of me confounded yoga posture as a pointless exercise and culture for people to meet one another and look as if they were high-minded. Still I maintain this judgmental position for the majority. After meeting Babu I formally admitted that I knew very little of the state of mind that I wished to acquire. It is true I knew the word, it was everything else that escaped me. So I spoke of it as if it were achieved, in a way hoping that if I lived the lie and spoke from its mouth that the play would convene in proper order. In this pensive stupor I had not ventured out for anything but river gazing, sitting, foodstuffs and garbage cleanup since my arrival. As I began to realize, I was there for my own contemplative self and going places would only distract me. I had no interest in doing such things, and if life had some profound paradigm to show my ignorant eyes, I had missed it, drunken fun, bad yelling, shallow laughter, deep remorse; dualism. Shall we treat others with respect and dignity? If you love people, will people love you? Maybe it is only the personal satisfactions of one's own interpreted Karmas? Can one not find satisfaction in solitude? If one is truly happy then one should need nothing external. May I do most, may I do more than the others, I should do more than I expect, I should not do as I want others to be for I shall be without want, but then why write a book? I am a stubborn bastard and all my dreams were dieting. But if I was to learn the posture of yoga, I simply had to take a course. Only then would it be suitable to practice on my own. I went around but trusted nobody's motivations and had none to myself beyond this pursuit of happiness.

Sivani was once a medical doctor but retired early after he fell into a slight heroin addiction. He claimed that posture helped him to regain his mental and physical health. He wasn't a famous teacher nor was he well known, he was average and it seemed right. It was some moments we found, some moments to observe the behavior of man, a moment to separate the mind from body and body from self. Sivani's little studio along the water was it. How beautiful the body I mused awaiting the class, this machine that creates the profound "I," the female stomach and back with smooth lines from the flower and bird, nature round, pure like fire, the male hands and jaw for earth with lines of maple and stratified rock. I conversed with none of the students as they showed. I didn't want them to know me and I did not want to know them for I doubted the fact that explaining myself would gain me any ground. My interpretation of conversing is that it was quite inflammatory, its production disgusted me and I could hardly escape it alone.

After class I left fast without a sound and made my way over to the devraj café, an open place with small pebbles filling its open floor, looking over Laxmanjula. The far tables outside sat next to a cement wall that bordered the hill leading down into the Ganga where the blue-green water flowed. A good place for a parade but people let you be on most occasions. I ordered a ginger lemon honey tea and stared down at the bridge admiring the troops of Langur monkeys as they stole the colorful belongings people didn't keep close, and the people's reaction, so afraid of animals, so angry, here now a yellow scarf is taken. I relaxed my eyes and steamed a breath of tea to my face.

"May I join you?" A young-looking girl with golden-brown hair and green eyes wrapped in a cream cloth stood at my table. She was from the class. And of course she did. A pale color was about her complexion, though, malnourished almost. Her eyes looked to be searching for a place to rest. "It's so beautiful," she said, slowly looking out over the view, resting her chin in her hands. "Yeah, really, I'd like to die in a place like this. Not now, though." My eyes felt stoned from the asans.
"Have you gone in the Ganga?" "every morning" "Perfect, isn't it?" "Yeah, strange, we should float down the whole length of it." We laughed at such an improbability." Would you mind an observation?" she asked. "I welcome them." "You look a little bit lonely or pensive or something along those lines." "Yeah, my face, when it's idle I look pretty serious, all the time pretty much. When I'm not thinking it looks like I am thinking. Lucky I guess. But yeah, I've just been mulling over a lot lately, and that's probably why I seem distant." "Yeah, distant, that's a good way to describe it. Well, it doesn't matter, we're all doing our own thing up here." "Yeah, I'm stubborn. I'm attached to my own moron. You seem fine. So you like the practice of yoga?" "Yeah, I enjoy it, the culture of it here becomes a bit absurd. But doesn't

everything that gets on paper?" And then I asked why she was in India.

Who cares why people are where they are, only now matters, where you came from or go from there is nobody's business, not even your own. "A long story, sad, you know. I'll tell if you promise not to judge me." "Judgment is for the jealous. Fuck judgment. We'll trade stories if it makes you sleep better." "Maybe it would. Well, I came here with a few friends a little while back and we ended up thinking exporting hash from here to England was a good idea. We were caught pretty fast, didn't make too much, someone called us out. I was just released from a prison in Mumbai a couple weeks ago." "Fucking crazy, as a trip, the idea of this, it's endless. You're beautiful, you know. "She blushed and we sat for a little while. I had nothing to say about her experience, I knew nothing of it and had no more stupid questions to ask. "I got interested in the posture while I was locked up," she said. "I learned to speak Hindi as well, but all that's nonsense. I learned how to see there, to live, you know kanji? Two years and seven months, film-like, over time and time again." She almost seemed better off." I feel like I don't even know who I was yesterday. That's such a long time to be around for the sake of another's wish." "Yeah, the proud and the slaving, I would have lost who I thought I was if I was anyone before I went there, so I thank the papers that put me there. My parents are the ones who have the most trouble, imagine. I haven't seen them all the while, but enough of this, right? I'd rather not talk too much about it, a waste to dwell, I just thought you'd get a kick out of it." She pulled off a sad smile to make for a change." So, why are you here?" she asked.

Insignificant, my simple life, yet we know only what we've been given and have no reference to the dying grass on the opposite banks of the river. My water forgot me only once and I fired her."I don't know, I was that guy growing up who everybody thought didn't care but would somehow make it, so here, I'm here looking to find some sort of satisfaction with myself I suppose. I always did care, just a little too much maybe. I want to be free and I want to be in love with life, you know, I want to be still with what I know, I want to be shameless of my dreams and bring them forth into life. i do, now i do"She looked at me and smiled, stood up and did a little pirouette. "I love life, and life loves me and you, and we're all something special, you know, and we're all living free and there's just nothing we can do about that."Julia was character, just as Bajei. We spoke of love and what it meant today for the people of today, the oversubscribed impersonal love that stems from something unrelated to love entirely. It was the expectations of love we suffered. As she walked across the bridge she looked back with an easy stare and gently waved with her tiny rose hand. I never saw her in real life again, but I've often wondered what became of her.

The stranger calls you out from bleeding eyes, as you keep
moving.
Her danger calls you out from needing lies, as you speak
nothing.

　　　　Night came with dreams of normal days in my little room surrounded by that poor, dirty tourist town. I awoke next morning at sunrise and sat in meditation trying to catch a breath before the next came. I failed, I failed miserably at maintaining an unaffected mind. Here we go again. Mango, orange, muesli, and fresh curd from the local dairy shop, and a bit of mint leaf torn with the fingers and a crushed clove in the chai from the stall across the street. I no longer dined in the main house in the mornings. I had been distracted by a local man who sold the best dairy products in town, a pot-bellied sweaty santa of a man who sold the most delicious sweets and curd. I made a good thing out of collecting my breakfast with him after my run. I would run up a hill I found a ways away until a path showed on the left side, leading to a waterfall in the hills. I dreamed there of isolation and that is what became of me. I went to those falls every morning alone before breakfast. I ran higher and higher until I was close to vomiting. When I regained my body I sat on a limestone boulder that looked over the town. Up there, on occasion thoughts evaded me entirely, other times everything at once came upon my brow making it impossible to realize from where the robbers had come. Lifetimes of dreams, lifetimes, now, I'll never have to live, a tasty present thought.

The course finished as soon as it had begun. It had lived only for a short while. Sivani was a fine teacher, when talking he would look away, but when your eyes drifted from his face he glared at you in a strange way. He spoke with his fingers but not his hands. "Do like this, not like this, why like this?" he would say, gesturing his fingers. Now, after the course, I knew some asanas and felt confident to practice. I had to do something with my time, other than act as the terrible analytical desk clerk of thoughts in youth. From what I hear, men go mad when you flip the mind like so with force and force again. I accepted this lifestyle and thought it well as a fate satisfactory until the end. I pressed flowers, picked up garbage, meditated, thought on the subject of all in the top room nightly, and sang Sanskrit songs I did not understand. I was content here but had no idea that I was. Something in me wanted more.

When I was younger I always wanted more, more excitement, more food for thought, and so I got removed from a few schools for being electric. The people by which my youth was ruled sat me in rooms trying to discover how I could become more suitable for them. All these tangible goals we've set for our selves under imaginary circumstance. We falter in our stance to discover who it is that is experiencing this world. We do not water the seed but cut the branches. In the hurry for moneys and the escape from ourselves, we lose our true selves and become only what we think should be so. Ruled by the mind we discard heart logic. We stay the same ever changing as if we were more comfortable this way.

Kernels of useless words
Annals of clueless words
Nonsensical unconnected sense;
hence, these incomprehensible words.

Smoke was all around in the morning and the days were particularly warm, wildfires raged round Rishikesh. When the sun went down you could see flames climbing hills in the distance. People would get stoned and watch the blaze from the cafes and talk about the inevitable combustion of everything, of somewhere and whatnot, very deep stuff. I was alone on my porch watching the people go about. I set down a depressing Kafka and tea I had been nursing for a go at the falls. From there I could look over the smoky town and reflect. The trails were aflame from backfires set up by locals. Every once in a while a burning log or hot stone would tumble down the hill. I swam naked in the upper tier of the falls pools, only for a cool-off, then returned fast to the road. I moseyed down to the usual cafe on the Ganga, a bit disappointed at the trails for being on fire. The air was thick with soot. I sipped another tea and watched a family of Rhesus Macaques fight over popcorn stolen from a tourist. A snake charmer on the stairs beside the cafe entertained a lone child, the snake swayed round and the child laughed and clapped his wrists together like a yell for the breast.

"Harri om, Prem." Bhodi smiled and placed his orange bag on the wall beside me."Bhodi, good to see you, just saw another orange cloth thinking it was you. How's the goings?""It's going well, how are you, how is living?" "Very well. Content. Just got back from the falls." "Be careful of the fires." A silence was with us as we looked around at the hills. " Prem, you must come with me to meet my friend Bhupi today. We're going to check out a piece of land I'm interested in purchasing. I want to make that ashram I told you about. Would you like to come?" I sat at the cafe waiting for the time to pass. Bhodi pulled up in the front of the dusty hostel beyond the stairs. I ran up and took a seat. It was a silent ride up to Jara road then down into lower Rishikesh. Not too far from here I would frequently find myself passing a man who had ingested too much Detura, an alkaloid based intoxicant; he had come to visit a long ways before, an accountant, now he rested in a bed of rubber tires chewing on a wooden block. His face has deformed to accommodate that block. An old private tourism office was close by, and we parked the Ambulance along the wild cannabis growing along the roadside. A well-shaved dark man with green eyes and an uneven stance stood out front waving his arms. He shook hands with Bhodi, then myself. Bhupi. An old friend of Bhodi's. He would be driving with us to see the property under consideration for contemplative use.

"I advise you try the lassie I like of the north," he said. He knew well. We walked around the corner and came to an old rundown shop the color of rotting lime. A few stainless steel benches lined the inside, a table rested in the center with a bucket of spoons atop. Flies buzzed to the face but we did not care. A dirty thin boy with a Zapata mustache kind of threw us a glass each from the bar. The milky drink held such a dynamic flavor that I became sad I had done so little to invest my time in discovering the secret streets. I was truly a moron. They made the lassie a day before then let it sit in a freezer so the fat could float to the top creating a hardened layer they garnished with almonds and raisins. The sweet sunk to the bottom. Opposites fall into place if you give them time, together they're so delicious. We finished and started off for the dam crossing that led to the other side of the river. "Have you seen the butterflies, Prem?" asked Bhupi.
"I have not," I had to say, but soon I would, I would be walking up the Riba one afternoon with an overused head. The pink swarm that rested on the rocks would look like a Banksy of the wild. There now they fly out all together spraying the air. Those dancers will save my life and conclude the last speck of disenchantment.

The mist of color has yet to come upon me, my wonder sits
unsaturated.
My thirst for color has yet to run beyond me, my slumber sets
suns elated

An old road partly paved and partly dirt led us through
an elephant sanctuary, the outskirts to the national park. Bhodi
spoke of all of the sahdus and wandering people living in the
forest that were forced to leave. The bastard suit has turned over
even the hidden stones. Only the Gujars remained, an old
wandering Muslim sect that gained their rights through internal
means of support. They had small temporary structures in the
place labeled "Park" and wandered from place to place with
livestock and supplies. A true forest dwelling people. Man has
sold and cut trees before they are trees.

We arrived at a pocket-size village by the name of
Ghadughat. It was up a thin meandering river that led into the
Ganga a ways down, the Riba. It was an agriculturally based
town; fields of wheat on parcels of land were divided by old
waterways. Simple homes made from stone stood on a corner of
each of the lands. Bhupi led us down a small path into the fields.
Each family we passed by stared at us on friendly terms, an
Indian business man, a bald white Swami, and a young blond
guy walking the fields of rural India. Out of a house came a
lanky countryman. He ran towards us, when he reached us he
shook Bhupi's hand furiously. His name was Rawat. He shook
Bhodi's hand as well and then my own and gave a big smile, his
teeth specked with tobacco he had been chewing. He invited us
up to his house for tea and sweets.

Rawat would be brokering the deal for the land Bhodi
wished to acquire. Rawat was the mayor in a way, elected by
way of passage, almost like Rawat is the loudest and most
friendly so he must be mayor. On the turn he also owned the
largest parcel of local land.

Yaks and a cow sat chewing large leaves in an open stall next to Rawat's house, the old crumbling farm, dark without electricity, blackened from the fires. Four chairs were placed by a woman on a large cement patio in the front. The patio as well as the house were above the ground that the fields were on and held a view of the crops all the way down to the river. Bhodi, Rawat, and Bhupi began speaking Hindi, and from what I could determine they were talking about the land and the local government. I was there enjoying the scene, watching the men and then the fields and then the other things. Out from the low doors emerged Rawat's wife and two daughters. His wife carried us a plate of four teas, the elder daughter held a tray with bright cloved ladu. It seemed the younger of the daughters had come outside to feed curiosity. "Namaste," I said. The girls giggled. One had only recently become a women, the other was a bit more senior. Both were dark and beautiful without the world upon their long hair and big brown eyes, each wore a sari, green and blue. They were something, these seraphim, and what was I to them? Country love, I was not invited. Could I have been there with them? We sipped the tea and ate sweets. The clown at the party of tears.

Rawat's wife was a well behaved country woman and did not speak up with men around. We bowed for her tea and started down along the cement waterways to the land. A barking deer called from across the river, "Minang." Bhodi bent down and reached to the ground beside the waterway and pulled up some green leaves."Watercress," he said.He would pick up wild plants and eat them. To acquire knowledge of local flora is no longer a given to us dependent addicts of delivery. Keep on, run, keep your eyes to the floor. Neither Rawat nor any of the other townspeople had known that the plant was edible. A funny scene in the poor town absent of food with food just before them, still it is of no use.

After a little time down the waterway we came to a parcel of land that looked to be abandoned for many seasons. Thorny bushes waist high covered the ground, within were blue and orange wild flowers, green ferns, and yellowing cannabis. A few old trees sat on the property, a hand friendly tree of mango lived near the edge of the land close to the river. The rear of the property went right up to the neighbor's plot, the sides as well, corn. The front led all the way down to the riverside where it met with a boulder on the water's edge. Bhodi whispered to me with excitement that he would make a platform on the top of that boulder, for postures and contemplation. He said that one day he was going to get the money to purchase this land and build rooms for people from all over the world to come and be at peace.

I let the three men talk and wandered over to the boulder to rest on its top. There I watched the river go by with some fish. I felt I could live there and wished I had. Workers collected stones from the riverbed and placed them in satchels worn by donkeys. A spliff.

We thanked Rawat. His daughters waved at us from the fields a ways off, baskets of leaves balanced atop their heads. Love. We walked back along the waterways. The drive along the roads through the forest back to Rishikesh invited me to dream of a life in the country. The carless till, the ode to season, a motion to leave the chains behind. Bhupi, he asked me all about my life, really a life undetermined. He was surprised a young man would be traveling all by himself. Why would I want to be so alone, he wondered, why I was not married without a desire to do so. I threw him to an odd place. I enjoyed Bhupi at first impression, he was one of those guys who's blatantly genuine, god fearing but almost in a satirical way, poking fun at his own self on the regular. His right arm was noticeably larger than his left due to neglect, all in the name of Hindu etiquette. They dropped me off back in town. I would meet them again around the cafe, we would return to Ghadughat another time when it was right.

Back on the land of V's, I sat in my room with a book until dinner, dialogues with Sri Nisargadatta on the true nature and timelessness of being. Fascination or timid regression, an aspect of perceivable truth. He smoked all day and knew only bliss. A man found him, he did not find men. I put off the book and started my way to the main house. I walked slowly through the gardens, picked and ate a marigold, and looked out over the river. A newborn Langur monkey played on a branch nearby. I started over to the door and rang the bell. Mohan greeted me. He looked alive no matter the hour, he took me in and offered tea. We exchanged words of some kind and I guess I needed to move around. My mind said that I was useless and wasting away. Bang. I would walk to the Vishwanath temple on a mountain westward. I would sleep there for an evening. Vanamali entered, looking as if she had just come out from the void, her eyes stoned and her walk slower than usual as if with clouds. She seconded the notion that I go to Vishwanath. It had a view and the temple was simple and quiet, no white would be there. It was a character I wished to be, I looked to be. But don't we all feel so special?

Dew was all around in the morning. I awoke to the sunrise bell. With me were enough supplies to suffice a journey: rolled oats, dried apricots, almonds, bread, peanut butter, water, some blankets and a sleeping bag. I put it all in a rucksack. I closed the wrought-iron gates behind me and went off. Walking along dirt roads I got out of the town. I watched the sun slowly come into the small village above. People moved about in the streets getting to their day. They smiled at me, they didn't cost me anything. The trail got on and the houses became more scarce. I stopped at a creek crossing and sat atop a log to eat my breakfast. A company of parrots fed from a mango tree. Did the parrots resemble the mangoes or did the mangoes resemble the parrots? I didn't know which was so. I continued on. The trail led me through the valley of the hills and then up and around. I felt good doing something on my own. Don't we have to do something? The earth was lurid and the plant life around me was born of a deep green. A place to which I had longed to return, I was struck by a certain familiarity. Man alone in the forest, especially home, easily achieved. The jungle book, the savage. The imagination, wasn't it? I took a break on a high ridge and could see off in the distance what looked to be a temple, the white structure with something like flags fluttering around in the wind. I took some water and almonds. I wrote to the page.

He has no mentor, only enemies, no waving only static. He knew them best for they were his friends and would never harm him. Only fear drove them mad to kill one another. The adoration came from fears frown. The monkey's crown; page dear, once more I have let you down.

Four men came walking by, carrying with them a water pump supported by planks of wood. They rushed passed me and yelled some vulgar joke in Hindi and smiled like stoned grazing cattle. I walked on. The trail turned rocky. I lost my way and was doubling back some until a young boy with a bundle of sticks under his arm came to my side. "Follow me," he said with his hands. We walked in silence. He stopped in the front of me and motioned to the ground, and we both sat on a smooth rock and had a view of Rishikesh below. He pulled out a paper package the width of two fingers and the length of one. He removed a Beedhi. The tendu leaf goes for the paper, inside some tobacco. He offered one. He lit the ends with a wooden match. He placed the flaming item in my fingers, and I waved it out. We smoked there and I looked in the sky.

The boy was more of a man than I, he must have been in his early twenties. He had perfect bowl cut hair, big teeth, and a quick worker's smile. He gifted me the rest of his smokes by placing them in my front pocket and returned to walking. I

followed him for a while longer, until we came to an old village
where with his hands he made it clear that I must go to the left
and that he would be going off to another place. We parted with
some gestures and I went on with the sun lowering into the
afternoon. A second town showed itself and I could see the
Temple above from there. Small schoolchildren were out playing
cricket, they hollered as I passed and danced their most
provocative western jump. I continued on and came upon a long
stairwell that led up to the temple. The top was windy with flags
clapping and the air was colder than below. A three-sixty view of
the world. To the north, the Himalayas. to the southeast,
Rishikesh, to the west open hills and a large town I could only
partly make out, Mussuri. The temple grounds were simple, a
mandir was in the center of its paved ground with a large brass
murti of Krishna inside. A fat pujari sat giving prayers in lotus.
His quarters were off to the side and the largest building stood
beside it serving as a room for fire ceremony, it had a grand open
fire-pit.

Two guys sat on the steps leading up to the temple
chewing pan. As I looked their way they smiled and waved for
me to engage them. Chandra and Virochan. They took care of
the place, they were from Rishikesh. They knew of the Vanamali
Ashram, and were happy to know I had walked my way on the
trail to visit the temple. As always an arati would be held at the
setting of the sun, I should go to that, afterwards they would
introduce me to the pujari. I left them and found a seat by the
southwest wall to watch the sun. I took out a sheet from my bag,
covered my cooling body, and made myself a peanut sandwich.
A good time for a joint, I smoked and the sun set twice. Sitting in
silence cross-legged, a hint of freedom, my bed is filled with the
women of Gustav Klimt. The pujari approached and asked from
where I had come. He knew of Vanamali and had spoken with
her before. "Where do you plan on sleeping this evening?" he
asked. "Anywhere, maybe outside, do you have any place?" He
smiled and told me that he figured as much. "Sleep in the temple,

where the fire ceremonies are held. The two groundskeepers
sleep in the fire room as well and they can fix some dinner." He
left for his house.

Chandra and Virochan humorously deformed their faces
as if in freezing cold when I walked in the main building. They
stoked a fire below ground level with a long stick. They pointed
to the floor in room's corner, a place to rest. I laid out a cloth bag
and sat alone for a moment. Profoundly aloof, I knew not the
feeling from when I was younger, the perpetuated. People my
age were in their first year of college enjoying days filled with
debauchery and young American girls. Here I was in India, alone
on a cold mountain, warming my hands in a cheap bag atop a
stone floor, doing things I thought to be of value or of none at
all, fuck it's all the same, the celibate monk still acquires syphilis
in the end, the dark side. Scared that I had thrown myself to the
wrong side I was pulled into darkness and felt the air deserved
not my breath but the consumption of fire. How can one truly
know emotion? Is the misunderstood Skinner's box an answer,
these other sensical evaluations? Or may we delve so deep into
the mind as to sit in that place from where thoughts arise, wrap
our hands around the clay from which they dance and then
become finally this which we gaze upon. The youth decides that
he had not a person to relate to and I even called myself selfish
for thinking such thoughts. I threw them out on the floor and
wandered over to the fire where dinner was being prepared.

Due to my basking in negativism, my two new comrades
noticed my depressed state. So nice when we are able to feel the
people around us and act accordingly. "Cheer up," they said, and
passed over a clay chillum they had made themselves. It lit up
and went back and forth, back and forth, back here forth there. It
was packed a second time and passed around some more. We all
sat stoned watching the fire. Virochen leaned over to me and
whispered,"Nassha Prem ha?" He spoke with a bit of Hindi."Ha
virochen, nassha." Nassha meant stoned."Why did you come

here to mother India, Prem?" he asked authoritatively. I put my
index finger to my temple for thought. "I suppose my father
really, but now it seems, and seamlessly, that I'm looking for
something to set me free, Virochen.""Looking, what are you
looking for?" Chandra asked.I laughed. The three of us began to
laugh. "Myself, but it seems I am right here.""Yes, Prem, you are
here, always here. Where did you go before?" Virochen yelled
sarcastically."Nowhere, Virochen. I have been here the whole
time, my fucking mind is stolen each day I swear, like a bipolar
child I am, it seems I do not yet know why I have come to
mother India, nor this earth on which we rest""Ah, this earth,
difficult, yet more simply, here, you have come to meet us,
Prem," said Chandra."Yes, yes, here to see us," said Virochen.
"Ek or chillum.""Tk, tk," said Chandra."Dinner smells good." I
said"Kicherie Prem.""Oh, very good.""You like spicy, yes?"
Virochan asked."I've heard through the jokes that it makes your
semen sweet."
They fall to the ground from humor."This may explain why the
American women like us India men so much." Chandra laughed
and peed his pants just a drop.
"How about you, Chandra, how do like the life?" I asked "I don't
know, I come to work, work three months, go home one week. I
eat good, I have work in the temple, I have my family."

        We spoke about family and respect and love as well.
They wanted women, scantily clad women. But all these things
didn't matter then, it was the principles behind them that were
important if at all. Family itself seemed a useless tribe mentality,
like related strangers we appreciate more than the next. Respect
was only as good as the sincerity behind it because empty words
are spoken betrayals to the self. Love was an endless discussion
the chillum would not allow. So we took another and ate
kicherie. Rice mixed with nuts, vegetables, and spices. After
eating they demanded to hear the young man's account of
western sexcapades. I saw my own experiences as menial and
wished to be naked with other naked bodies, free. There were

places like this but I had not the power to throw away my search
for the perfect stance before it was made. I left them and
returned to the floor. In the night during dream, a dream came
that I have had on numerous occasions. It starts sailing through
tunnels lined with clouds, so peaceful and warm, almost an
orgasm but never a wet dream came of it. Suddenly out from the
void these clouds quickly shard, then the whole place vibrates
me to death, which awakens me to life. The texture of the dream
stays with me. I sleep. Virochen and Chandra slept beside me,
they cuddled with one another. Both had wives, the body is
nothing, I cannot fathom the fact.

Temple bells rang in the sunrise. I left from the temple
and sat below an old pine bordering the property. The sun came
out of the mountains. I smoked the air. The Pujari came beside
me. "Come to sit?" he asked. We sat below a statue of Krishna,
the humming oms residing within. Some prayer jabber came and
I knew the words, still I sat in silence. In my time I have had no
belief in idolatry nor organized religion. It frightens me to know
so many men can go after killing the same man without reason.
The mind is equally as horrifying, yet alone in killing, at least we
can be responsible for our own murder. I hear, do not search, but
sit in the cessation of searching, the color for all man, enough
man. We sat until the sun was high. We left the temple with a
final prayer and a prostration to the cosmos. The both of us sat
on a bench outside along the west wall. "If you find yourself
with free time, venture up to Ghadughat," he said. "A myth or
something like it states the Shiva has once gone up there and
fallen into deep meditations, and it was some boulder and a cave
he chose to use for sitting." I told him nothing of my recent visit,
and we are now myth.

Virochan and Chandra laid out on the stairs leading
down the mountainside. They gave big hugs before I left. "Be
love with India, Prem," Chandra said. I had known them for so
little a time but they were honest friends. I gave them my

remaining almonds, and in return they gave me the clay chillum. I walked off and the temple grew smaller in the distance. I went on absent until near the end before entering the boarders of town, I checked a mango tree. From its branched arms hung mangoes the size of my hands. I climbed up and grabbed two, fresh for eating. I sat devouring them, aware of monkeys in the forest. Messy, for there is only one way for me to properly eat a mango, throw manners to the wind, dive headfirst, and devour each and every sweet and tangy morsel. Where is there room for man's manners in the forest?

While with the fruit, from no place at all a young looking sadhu approached. "Might I join you in this feast?" he asked. "If it was my feast to have, maybe it would be me that you could invite." I cut him off a piece with a sharp hunting blade and he crouched beside me. From his bag he pulled a picture of himself taken from when he was in college. He had been out only for a short time but the outdoors had taken their toll on his body. He had long dreads and a smooth black beard, he wore only a dhoti. He told me of his journeys; he had walked all around the hills for some years. He was now returning to Rishikesh to see a doctor about an infection on his left foot. He was the meaning of Sahdu and I kept him in my mind, almost an Indian Adam wandering the earth with the innocence of a child but the education of a scholar. He spoke. "We are the conscious ones, and it will be the universe that realizes itself, but even in knowing this I stumble with such sadness, the dark corners of peoples fear" He went on and I think of Polonius "To expostulate why day is day, night is night, time is time were nothing but to waste a day, night, and time." Quite so, but my day had yet to finish. Pillage lands and you may find resources, pillage the mind and you shall find your truth. Besides it is more fascinating for me to waste these times, days, and nights disregarding my respect for the three, for just off the earth these things are nothing, we are but stardust settling.

The streets felt good, the ashram home, and my room a familiar cave. Vanamali and Mohan saw comedy in my desires to wander but kept that to themselves. We had dinner and I told them of my walk. I could walk all the way to the Himalayas if I pleased. That night came a good dream. A scene of Tolstoy's father Sergius, A comical cliche. I had been along with him, Sergius. Near the end, when he was wandering as a sadhu like man. He was still confined to the rules that he set and his fingers seemed useless anyways.

The dusk peels me naked so I stay wide awake grateful and
complacent along the light lines from the sun escaping day.
The husk kneels before me naked so I play awake not wasteful
nor defiant along the light lines from the sun scraping day.

Boys from the ashram had this day off. Only a few words were said in passing since my arrival. After taking breakfast one of them asked me to join them up-river a ways for the afternoon. Good guys, students of yoga, energetic. We left for the path that led along the ashram walls. They brought me through to an orphanage where some of their friends lived. I saw a sprawling garden thick with dark manure where fresh produce grew by the hands of children. A yard for playing and plenty of rooms. It was rundown but not enough to deem it useless. A group of girls followed us as we walked through, they hid and laughed every time I turned around to see them. The boys I was with called up to one of the windows of the building. Another boy stuck his head out. He replied something, then came running down a set of stairs a ways off. He joined us and we walked on. A winding dirt road carved into the sides of the hills above the Ganga led us to a steep little path down to the banks. A beach, large boulders rested on either side. A still pool of easy blue water collected just beyond the sand, a stone upriver carved out an eddy. All we could hear were the birds and the water running past the rocks.

I sat out across the rocks. One of the boys grabbed a large stone from the banks and slowly walked into the depths. He shot up without the stone half way across the river. It was to see how far across the river one could get while being weighed down. Each of us could make it only about half the width of the river escaping with breath. The boys dried in the sun. They left off as I stayed behind.

In the sun I crouched on a water-cut rock in the center of the current. I pondered my short travels and felt they had been longer than they were. My time was fluid and remembering my future life brought laughter upon my lips. I am to fathom the minutia of the peoples before I am to become a person. Remedies for sick roads I have yet to travel. Work. Woman.

I looked towards the beach and a young girl was undressing in the sun. She had long rusted brown hair and a body that looked to be crafted on the wheel of a lonely man. I dreamed she might swim over to where I was. She walked upriver a ways and floated down diagonally, effortlessly reaching the rock on which I dreamed. I am overworking the dough for simple acknowledgments of attraction. She sat beside me. She had recently been released from the army and had found her time with the land most impressive. This way was about her, anonymously pococurante in movement. We exchanged nothing from words, the language of the body is far more filled with brilliance. Her feet lay disposed in the water, her hands slowly danced about her sides. She smiled with her head down, her reflection fluttered in the ripples. I admired what she was, what I was with her, and what she did without me. She leaned over, turned her head and kissed me on the lips, and then she pushed herself off into the water.

I was smiling to the sun when she floated on her back beyond the eddy into the still pool. She sang for me to join her. I let off the rock to the water and swam towards the shore that dropped fast. She had crawled halfway onto the riverbank and was lying up with her feet below the water. I reached her and lay out looking to her eyes. I kissed her, then moved my head back but kept my eyes with hers. Again our lips met absent of affliction and now our bodies bonded. We rolled in the sand and got into one another. Nothing became of us, only something seamless in exchange for soulless profundities. Sounds of river came and went, the birdsong sang. The nudes rolled without a thing to take. Heavy heart beat in the warm air, and I was alive. The love of flesh; infatuation of the meats. If only I could find my illusive true love, but with the meaning lost the host had absconded with my reason.

After these charades we lay there in arms with legs intertwined. It was a long while in the sun and without a thing spoken. It was about the dusk feeling during summer after a hard day of work. It was only clarity, but the rarity of brave sexuality frightened me. We gathered our clothes and walked from the beach back up to the trail. We held hands looking around like virgins. A tea at the devraj cafe and we each had a bidi from the mountain boy on the steps nearby, before I left off for yet another dance to judge. I planned to meet her the next morning. She kissed me slow before I walked up the hill back home. I had killed a matador and walked with proud shoulders. In my room I sat free of attributes. What was there now to worry when all my desires were to be satiated. I was the prefabricated happy, only five easy payments of fuck yourself harder. To be as free as this; Neomarica. I slept well that evening, a dreamless sleep, I do not know the place I traveled but when I awoke I was still there.

Before the dawn I jogged to the falls to make do with a practice of asan. By sunrise I was swimming in the upper pool, diving down deep holding my breath. A white crab played in the sand. With a great deal of liquidity I strode on back to the cafe. There she was, as beautiful as the day before, even sober eyes dream. Sun kissed the purple flower in her hair. She was leaving to Delhi. People come and people go, moments pass so quickly without us if we're without you. There is no room for defying shoals of beauty in this ocean of madness. For the morning we discussed what we figured the life was about, or what it isn't and whether or not one should even speak of such things. Before she walked off came only an embrace.

I sat on an old stool in the bookstore beside the bridge, reading over a book of Jared Diamond's. A review of mankind's last thirteen thousand years and why its civilizations have been affected in the ways they have. Bhodi enters the bookstore and sat at my side."Hari om, Prem." He placed his hand on my shoulder"Hari om, Bhodi." "Prem, I have acquired the necessary funds for that property, easy, all the dreams are well." He smiled."What a way to do things. I had a feeling you'd get what you wanted. Now you can get out of here and commit your mental sepuku in the forest," I said with a smirk."Yes, mental suicide indeed. But I was thinking you could go live there until I move, set up the place, warm the locals," he offered, knowing the answer already.I weighed my options for no time at all. "I would like nothing more. It seems as if a change is necessary anyway." "You can stay there, then, get the place started. There's a great room for rent beside the property. Get to know the town and its people. You'll do well out there, you'll like the seclusion and the town is getting busy with style anyhow." We laughed.
"Yes, we be the giddy white man seasons. When shall I move?" "As early as tomorrow, Prem, why not, yeah. Wake up, the world is on fire!" He said that often. His father used to say that to him when he was a child."This way then, why not," I laughed. "What a character you are." We are the characters, we are the chosen ones.
> Your from under ground the sun.
> The subterranean pacina.
> The naked bathing ones mangling la vida.

The world may invite you to be no one, but what a grand lie to think that the janitor in Grand Central Station does not cry when his wife becomes crippled and can no longer feel the embrace of his calloused hands. I would have all my belongings ready by the land of V the next day before noon. I thanked Vanamali and Mohan for letting me room with them in such peace. They spoke eruditely on the subject of being. The old know more of time and its nature. They gave me good footing to become interested, they taught me by example how to sit, and I was afforded a place to try my hand at some postures. "Be careful of the world and its violent cards," Mohan said with a wink. Vanamali spoke with a soft yet stern eye: "Be weary of desire and temptations, beyond your walls lies a wild world." Just like Cat Stevens used to say before he was stolen by the book. Her purple sari, a perfect tone of maternity. "Learn what you see but do not pay much attention to the townsmen, they have been left backwards," Mohan warned. Was I sad to leave? I thought, *No, I am to move forward, or around I suppose, is there no position at all?* We ate one last dinner, a great classical seven course meal.

In the night, in my little room so calm, it smelled of incense and fruit and I had made it my temple. I had dreams of the day, dreams so real with nothing abstract or uncharacteristic of the reality I had created. It seemed as if I never left awake. Still I awoke to the sunrise bell again and sat for meditation with the two of them. Lost in thought I found little silence, a vast scope of ideas and fortune like goals, radically aimless, puked about my head. I waited by the wrought-iron gates with my belongings. Bhodi pulled up in his ambulance. These parents of mine wished me a safe stay around, and let it be known that I should stop by whenever I had the free time, I would always be welcome. We drove off for Ghadughat.

When the whalebone buttons matter no further, these ones are aright.
Now in passing with passion filled fright, say what you were singing in the night.
When the smokes were gone and we ran far into the fight my love.
When the jokes lent dawn and we'd spanned all the lands up above.

Ghadughat

Chapter Three

A jungle sick with thinking: the green and simple Ghadughat. My first night alone in the country was moonless and a million stars shown above the village. I lay in this home I was given, built years before by the community. An easy cement structure square in shape. A half-kitchen was off the main room, some built-in shelves took up the walls. Two steps led to the chipping red front door where the light shown through the day. The whole outside of the place was an off-white, a good something off a Gogh from a distance. A path led through the garden in the front down to a group of young mangos, and cannabis grew all around. The Riba flowed before me. Below the stars by the moving water with no moon within; I combusted to fame and fortune. To grow old with dreams unfurled and complete but all the same if I died right there and then without a story told. In these friends, so profound and still, slow love of the arbitrary. Why would one convene to play in this heartless race which we see so clearly? Duty is a farce, I thought, desire an illusion, and the true ethos of America. Our love only Eros arising from pains and fear. I sat with the company of stones until a darkened silence wide and full of space took me wayward. I lost the mind and my way with all the other things. They chopped off Victor Jara's hands for singing what his heart knew to be true.

Jingling- jangling. Entering. Left.
Tinging-tangling. Leaving. Theft.
Squeezed in the night with these warmed windy wakeful tones
lazying along these trees slammed with a light's width strung
worn from whimsical moans.

Shush. Shush, hear, there the tingling trees dance across the throne.

An amla tree sat in the corner of the property, a chair hammock hung from its low branches. I read books there, nestled in a valley beside a river and its working peoples, who seemed so enraptured with this role they played bemused. And I looked around periodically struck by brief spells of inadequacy. I felt it necessary to shed a bit of light upon my ignorance. The desperate ignoramus. Come hither, Steven Hawking, Hofstadter, Zinn, Darwin, Russell, and others. They lead no place satisfying, just as the high. Nowhere to go with perceived information, fuck; these genius peoples, what must we know? You categorical maniacs. Yes I have at least conformed my mind a bit more than it was before. Even if this book does not suit me in the end, I have organized my brain that much more just by writing it, and you there, by reading it.

Sadar, the caretaker of the property on which I stayed was a story I came to know. He was a lewd man with missing teeth and a heavy alcoholic, the one that deserves company, abstracted, just as all the rest, waiting about the earth, as if placed in a theater. The confident marionettes. He was a tiny man and could be commonly seen wearing a stained kurta pajama a few sizes too big, often with his passed-out wrinkled face slapped down in the dirt. His daughters played out front in the garden. They would peek into my room and run off when I went to greet them. A shy couple of girls, and I was their John Smith. Sadar's wife, Sajani, was a lovely woman with a country mind, always working. She taught me how to cook chepatti over an open fire below her stairs and always gave me strange looks when I jogged through town towards the hills.

As you reach for me your highness. The nature comes uninterrupted, these tiny repetitive lovely livings grasping without grip; suckling any flower- they are fine without me.

These days alone with country went by like dreams in light. Low, green grass lined the riba's shore, right above where the round stones hung around, smoothed shiny from their journey down the mountains. I slowly wade through a pool of clear water. I spied the bird I came to know. I sat atop a boulder to enjoy it. I never found the bird's name. It had the royal blue like the kingfisher wore and a white belly with a black line along its chest. The tail was longer than the whole length of its body, and it flew with great ease fluttering up and down. *Symposium* was on me,I had read it that week, *Phaedrus* as well.

To convene with the greats, you myths of the future, you fallen heroes with whom we saunter through life. Even in our entire era based upon secondhand knowledge you suffice as if you were real and are in fact here now. They described a world without the use of obtuse doxologies, with simple words, and nothing at all, nothing our infantile human minds could ever hope to describe and understand with this limited and archaic language. I am awed. To know, to know nothing at all, falling in and out of love with the ideas that sit you down. My thoughts came from another point, echoes. The inebriated nudes, can we have understood what anybody has truly felt? Alone on a pedestal of this greatness we claim comedy. The love figure, a legend of squalid interpretations, the Buddha and compassion from Christ, words as tooth and maw. Funny, alone, pouring over this one and that, Himalayas. Sip wines from a kylix around all the philosophers, playwrights, and theologians, get to the bottom of the simple things before you bash this man before you. To be busy living some type of life void and abundant of thought. Have we already defined ourselves as character in this business of the show, could we have done this? My peers, what are they worth? Am I worth a thing to them? I was there empty, and only I alone could conjure this plethora of advance, but is conjure even the right word? I begin to question my diction. There I was in the river and my good bird had flown out of sight.

With ease your spools of travelers do hop on through the stones.
You please sore pools with travelers to stop through and
condone.
I say now River, it is you I cannot see.
I no longer have a giver; Oh do please implore your spools to
travel on with me.

Rawat, the man who sold Bhodi the plot of land,
oversaw the migrant workers that cleared the wild growth. He
was a loud man and once he saw his way it was hard to change
it. He came by my door one morning and took a seat on the
stoop; I came outside and he patted me on the thigh. He laughed
in my company, then motioned for me to follow him. We walked
down over by the riba, to the boulder that lay huge at the foot of
the land. Beside it was a small pool of water shin shallow. On
the sandy banks he took his right hand and drew a small vein of
the river dammed by stone. The hand with which he drew was
missing all but two fingers, his thumb and pinky. He'd blown the
other fingers off with a small piece of dynamite while trying to
kill fish in this river, instant karma. He had drawn a suggestion.
He thought it good to dam up a portion of the river for a bathing
ghat.

A fine idea. Rawat yelled something in Hindi towards
the direction of the fields. Out from a low brick hut an old
leathery man with enormous strength on his body came running.
He was a dark Nepali, covered by sun. He wore a black beanie, a
pair of navy blue shorts, and a torn white button-down. Bahador
they called him, worker. He knew nothing of English but was a
lively man, and moved his body for my words. He was a drunken
fool when he had the money. When he didn't, he kept a smoking
bidi in his mouth. Rawat offered me some of the tobacco he
chewed. Bahador jumped into the river and began moving stones
from the bottom of the pool to one side, making the beginnings

to a wall. I jumped in, and together Bahador and I moved stones all day. Rawat left us; we splashed and made jokes with grotesque looking faces. We spent a few days moving stones. In the end we had a nice pile straight across a portion of the Riba, waist high that held back enough water to swim and bath in.

There was no work this day, there was never work any day. The property was cleared of its growth and looked larger because of it. Sitting in my hammock reading the seventh chapter of the *Bhagavad Gita*, a young aesthetic came to me. I had seen him before; he lived off a ways back from where I stayed in a low-lying stone house. He cooked outside, and the air he produced was heavy with spice. He spoke English well, but was humble and used few words to expound his thoughts. "There is to be a wedding, and you must attend." He handed me a red carrot. He was Rawat's cousin, and it was Rawat's daughter who was to be married. It would be a small celebration due to the fact that it was not an arranged but a love marriage, an act ill-accepted. You hear sometimes of the radicals that kill couples deviating too far from the path. They justify their actions as honor killings. Bhodi was not invited, as it is not customary for a Swami to be present at a wedding. The wedding was to start the following day. He gave me a wink and went off into the fields.

Walking through the corn, head high, I could see smoke and smell coriander and cumin drifting from Rawat's house. The wedding was to be a three-day ceremony. The first, a celebration for the family, mainly in honor of the father giving away his daughter and the dowry that goes along with it. Sadar joined my stride in the fields. "Prem, you want Indian marriage, do you not? I can find one for you to marry." He slapped his knee. "I do not think that I am ready for marriage, Sadar. When I am, maybe I'll come back and take you up on your word."
All the town was there, a small town, all dressed up. The yaks and cow were painted and decorated. Lights and banners hung from all over. A fire burned at one end of the patio lining the front of Rawat's house, and a group of women were sitting

around preparing food. A Gujarati drummed a clay pot with a piece of rubber banded tight over the top. Rawat danced within a small crowd, he had all the happiness of a child and his face glowed like the fire. The bride to be and women of the family gathered inside the house decorating themselves with mehndi, a henna like substance. I stepped near the dance and Rawat dragged me in. My traditional garwhal mountain clothes excited these celebratory drunks. I danced with him, and all the other men, arm-in-arm, turning in circles and yelling hooray. It was the moment for which they lived, for these men never knew old that night and never asked a thing from tomorrow. The colors stained our bored country eyes, and let us off into careless.

I danced until I could no further, then I stepped back and started for the fire. Rawat caught my eye and demanded that I go with him. He led me back into a room of his house. It was dimly lit by candlelight and a small fire that was going in a metal bowl on the ground, a charpoy bed lay beside it. Three men sat cross-legged on the floor chuckling, sipping whiskey from thin brass cups. Rawat led me to a cupboard in the corner of the room and did a dance in front of it. He opened it, gasped, then removed two bottles of mountain whiskey thick with glycerol. We do as we must. I would have drunk no matter, I wouldn't kid myself. He poured us both a quarter bottle, neat. Rawat linked our arms and gave me a grim filthy stare as we drank it all in a shot. Inebriated almost instantaneously, we returned to the festivities and could now dance forever.

I danced a ways home that evening, through the corn. I skipped along and smelled the turned soil. I sat on the low bank of the riba in the dark night and listened to the hills. A peacock called from downriver, "lou lou." I was free. Happy people. In my Shangri-La they knew nothing of the unreal and were content there thinking nothing more. There was nothing to find. I moved the bedding from my room up onto the roof of my little home and slept beneath the stars.

I awoke with the new sun touching my face, and my face touching a pool of vomit. It seemed that I had drunk more than necessary. Relieved I had not choked to death in my sleep, I washed off with cold well-water to the sounds of stones being stacked on one another. People of the town were constructing a new path from the road down to the river. I gathered the strength for a run and went off into the hills. A fox. I stopped in my tracks, as did he. "What is this man here?" he seemed to say. The fox and I both stared at one another. I admired it for a long while, it walks off.

Back by the house I did some practice down on the riverside. I was working on some breathing exercises when two young children came near leading a group of yaks. There was a pool close to where I did my practice and often watched the cleaning of the animals at this time of day. I took a headstand and watched the children as they laughed at me while washing their yaks. The meaning of asan escaped me, the body had run far. The Bride and groom met and were given to one another by each of the families. The bride was dressed in a luxurious pink sari. She was covered from head to toe in gold jewelry and intricate designs lined her hands. The groom wore a white tuxedo. They both looked good. I thought Rawat looked the most happy: proud of his daughter and finally a step closer to being free from children and dowry. His time to lounge was well overdue.

Sit like a child buying love, among racing displacements of speed and escape. Cheat like a child implying love, in these pacing arrangements we feed and sedate. Sit like a child crying love, in these dancing enchantments we heed to relate.

A seven-course lunch was served. Soft and crispy chapati and naan, a moist yellow green and red pulou spiced for the tongue, bryanis, classic hand rolled pakoras perfectly fried and rolled by the large women who eat, dhals of the rare beans, and much more I could not recognize. The delicious gujar hallvah was served, a sweet candied carrot dish topped with a layer of condensed milk. Everyone's clothes were stained by the end of the day from such a fest. We were always home. It was a joyous time. The night finished with live music. There was dancing and shouting. The last dance was made with the bride and groom. I gave my prayers to the new couple and gave Rawat a light slap on the nape. I walked home along the waterway and again slept beneath the stars.

The final day of the wedding was most emotional. Common to the country, when the bride is given away, she goes to live with the groom, wherever that may be, and most often the groom does not live near. Traditionally the bride will not see her family very much again. She may, but it is not common. All the town's men and women gathered in the small market area around the white neoclassical Fiat that was to take their friend away. The bride was getting her farewells from her family and friends. She was in a terrible state, crying aloud; tears flowed from her eyes and her makeup ran, but she had a smile that crept along the side of her lips knowing her path to womanhood had arrived. Rawat hugged her, then ran off into the crowd back home to hide his sunder. The taxi slowly drove off, children ran beside, flowers flew from the car. The music died. The wedding was over. The town grew silent, as if a parade had come and gone leaving only bits of color on the ground and laughter in the air. Days of silence followed the wedding. The town was tired. I took up reading the *Tou Te Ching*. The third most translated book after the *Bible* and the *Bagavadgita*. Way. Specifically attached to nothing, direction, perhaps the original direction before distraction or distinction. Thoreau attempted time by Walden pond. To be, to search for incumbency, to find the caste within, all the variables and sensical terms. I am true nature without words on the walls. Go live as the next man; fate with nonchalance.

I shan't own the city, nor shall the city own me, and what is this
place but a shanty town anyway? Arduously petty. They turned a
pretty penny. Wild Millionaires yelling across the plains. Silly
sorry games, but who am I to sauce this? Where is my Ferrari?

Continuously I looked upon the show of my atmosphere. The conglomerate encompassing all of which I have attempted to perceive. Bang. To dispose of individuality; the catch twenty-two; too easy to be the same. What am I if indeed I was never any other layered or displaced. Note, I may have been clouded all but none of my time. Nature aside. What is the difference? There I was and I had become of the surroundings, unmotivated happiness lined my days. The ride of the bodies of waters and salts. I hiked a trail to a cave trying to sit in these irrelevant thoughts. Something held me back from disappearing into the hills, though the thought came on numerous occasions. Leave the station and never return. Wander. Maybe this came from ego, but who defines the ego? Nietzsche? Freud? Who are these people to whom I lend my ear? If their collective consciousness be true, then may it swaft this mind away; be it false, no matter. I'll go now to fly as Icarus 'till my wings softly melt. Watch me while I fall into the oceans.

She told me to come in; so I am here.
I forget to introduce myself after passing on through the door; I
am no guest.
Feeling unwelcomed I write a poem from near the hearth.
I light a log with fire and then go scribbling to the air.
A spark comes free and burns the house right down to earthen
bare.
I had not time to warn a soul as the spark licked down my cape.

She told me to come in; this house I'd once escaped.

Bhodi approached on the riverside. He had driven in from Rishikesh. He was moving, moving to Ghadughat in some time. Well then to have the company of a monk and a scholar of the yogas. It numbed me to know my time alone was nearing its end. We walked upstream. We spoke of the difference between kindness and meanness. We found no difference yet compared them only to progression of human love, and what did that mean, we knew nothing. Lunch was taken on Sadar's roof that afternoon. We spent our time speaking of the weather and the beauty of the countryside. The unpeeled falling bark. Bhodi left off homeward; he was busy rummaging around the town.

Over at the local chai walla that pudgy garwhali kid who looked over the place was playing with his buddies. I sat in the low room below the street line. I sat on an old charpoy. A brute thin character of a guy walked in. Sitender, was his name. Sitender spoke and with his few words seemed to offer an out on feeling stale. I sip my chai with the colorful. Soon after he would show me pictures of the working women he and his friends had slept with. He showed me with such pride. It was beautiful, he loved and respected those women and would spend a good month's pay for their company. I finished my tea and made my walk back past the town and down the hill, where the jack fruit was starting to ripen.

I lay in bed with the door open to the river, a cool breeze coming through. Sadar knocked on the side of my door. "Come in, Sadar G," I said, knowing it was him. "Hari om, Prem G." He stood in the center of the room tickling his mustache. "Let us go to the house I know down the river."
I got up and went without responding. We walked on down to the riverside all along the path, through the yellow wild that grew then. Just a stone's throw away to a small hut built beneath a hill. I had seen the residents before, washing clothes in the

river, some of those long-haired freaky people. From afar the door was open, embers little light lit the inside. Through more flowers and cannabis we walked in and sat beside a man I had not seen before. He wore an off-white robe and had a long gray beard. His dreadlocked black hair wound up in a cylindrical form above his head. Another man lay on the other side of the room on a mat. He looked mad with blaze. An open fire burned in the middle of the room. The three of them spoke, they spoke something of me and what I had been doing there. Silence. The one most set for whatever it was that I wanted sat twirling bits of his beard between his fingers. He leaned over and pronounced good lines of high English."A pleasure to meet you, Prem.""My pleasure.""You've found this place." I was released with love from sleepy things gone by, what had become of me, sleeping lucky. The sun came and dew dried, still we were all the wiser. The chillum lit. Silence. Dusty smokes. The fire cracked, firing an ember to the face of Sadar. Deep laughter ensued. A woman walked in, tears beaded down her redding face. The robed man consoled her with a look toward her direction. Another woman entered; she too held a sadness. They fell into something easy and limp, prostrated to the man, and left. No mention came, was ordered or desired. A peace and more smokes went. The riba led into the Ganges, shallow now, the water growing warm, some slow moss coming. Monsoon would welcome back water, cooling with speed. I would enjoy that time; we seemed to love the land.

No matter how freedom is maintianed in this dark candor's dust.
It matters not a morsel, as even virgins take rust.

This man was a high-end commissioner in the state government. He had left running around. Fairy tales. A season after a British girl lived with them, the girl's father had tried to convince her of the home he so needed to believe. They left out for the Himalayas, I heard nothing else on the matter. I wished them well in the mountains doing as they wished to do. May they find what they are looking for.

Rishikesh all warm and fuzzy. I had gone to lend a hand to Bhodi. The mud roads leading from town were wet. The air was cold and the roads whyndy. An elephant showed itself to the road, and stood eating a good tree in the bend. Bhodi pulled the ambulance to a quick halt as a silence overtook us. The male elephant gently waved its tusks, white, and it didn't care about us. That free elephant eating by the road, Finally, it walked off into the wood. We went on towards the town. Just a ways down from the Sivananda compound a small path lead off the road down a steep hillside. Below, by the water's edge, little crumbled structures lay nestled in the forest of banyan . We walked down a long line of stone steps Bhodi's own hands had built. A hidden spot, removed from the dusty road above with loud air destroyed with a mess off things and people's ideas. I hung from a high branch above the temple site. Bhodi started building in the forest without the use of money. He left the organized monastic life, he had built a home, a temple, a guest house, and even a small boat that rested ashore. The forest department was aware of his presence but had not acted upon his removal. He kept to himself. One day a man across the river felt a white man could never deserve a plot on the holy river. Incessantly he demanded the police to remove the foreigner. One morning the departments came and destroyed the place. They removed his belongings and placed them under the custody of the forest department. He was cut down.

I remained. Bhodi did as well. He studied for the lectures he would be giving in Germany. I was there living with this flamboyant monk; at any other time it would have been troubling to accept. He longed to find a student. He dreamed to feel guru; disperser of darkness. You are guru. He laughed one day and admitted to having once slept with a horse. He concluded the animal must have enjoyed it. For the sake of doing things, he turned on Joseph Campbell's lectures on mythology and religion or lectures on Vedanta philosophy, the Greeks, symbology, at all times of the day. We wasted speaking, speaking of society, we saved ourselves by imagining our own Utopian concepts. What about them? Ripley's Brook Farm, the commune based upon self-reliance and other such things fell apart. The Fourier mood movements, purely led by arrogant minds, a grand idea ruined by idiotic conclusion-ism, the stubborn point of trouble. The Fruit-lands Utopia in Harvard ended in a spit of time. They felt they never missed out, they looked and found they looked for nothing, they had set out to make what they thought with no respect to what was. We were without lands complex with the over-communicated cycling self-reliance, love with boastful hits, the finis micro socius, hands of all, dancing on the earth with the beams of life scraping at our feet. The destroyers of Forbes. The witnesses of actions propelling our love with the courage to create without fear and hatred, violence and jealousy. Move not forever forward in circles.

-The iron winds of man that make this place run round, fool empires to stand in this place that we've not found.

As fast as you can see. Words spoken. I had this routine and lived by it, as Bhodi lived by his. The land had been cleared, now mostly female migrant workers camped out ready to begin the building process. Bhodi had spent some years studying architecture before wandering around the United States. He had written up a rough plan for the structure. I surveyed the workers. They began the septic tank.

Three women worked, one was pregnant but worked harder than the others. A man watched over them and cooked the meals over an open fire. I watched them from the rooftop. Three kids were in their company, orphans from Nepal. The day lit up their faces. They looked to be giddy with freedom from resolve, or perhaps worried sick with delusions. The man drove the shovel into dirt while the women helped lift it up with a rope when the head was filled. The remaining women carried plates of the earth to the other side of the land atop their heads.

Two weeks went by watching them. I offered my hand but to no avail, Rawat would refuse, I was to be doing other things. There were no other things, and it seemed I cared for nothing and when I heard myself speak. I grew tired before the end. Bhodi was busy conceptualizing some enlightenments, it didn't matter what he did. He had a good past with hallucinogens, the high effects of the sober view. When he thought he had strayed from a reasonable life, he started off to wandering America, reading various prophetic texts. A fan of the Grateful Dead, we listened in the sun on the roof. He spoke often on the Greeks and how he wished he had lived in their time. He was a tearing monk, as I presume he wished he lived what would be defined as a provocative life but could not find the island. So he settled for the one on the horizon. Like a child, I loved him.

Learning to walk comes without reason. For all things compared, walking is by far the best. To walk and be of nothing, to walk and become the lost of the land. The primordial ooze from which we have dispersed. To grasp a hand of earth. Along the river, by where the birds sing and the monkeys skip along the rocks. When in a place where man-woman-kind cannot be seen, combine your life and dreams to where the end bequeaths the start and you find yourself once more a child in the snow making angels down below. I learned to move my legs when I was young but learned how to walk only yesterday.

Bhodi offered a trip to the hills. We took the van out and drove far to where towns ended. Up in the heights we went to the shrines atop the mountain with a round view of all. A few men that stayed in the small rooms lined with beds with no space in between greeted us warmly. Fires raged along the ridges on dry grass and plant. As we walked along the paths we became aimless, and when we found ourselves we were surrounded by fire on either side. Wind blew embers past us and a heat came and went with the blows. Our faces went red with the light of burning. Silence without interjections of the current state. I danced standing still, a tiny animal with a head built for the stars.

Slowly the septic tank got finished. Some new workers came, an elder and two guys with them that went by the names of Baghat and Joti. They were only dreamers and looked to be not waiting but already there. We often swam together in the river and drew fish around to the small pools. The foundation made its way. More of the actor, more of the town. They knew me for what they knew me for and saw me sit on the roof at dusk. The kids no longer acted shy in my presence, they saw it as was what was and not what hadn't been before, familiar.

In the center of town I grabbed my water supply. I drank the groundwater until the well broke. The washer on the base cracked then loosened to crack the weld. I hurried up to the hillside to catch a Mahindra for the ride back along the winding cliffs. Time had passed without my realizing and the Mahindras had all gone home. I sat on a stone and ate a carrot. A truck pulled up with a long carrier in the back, the driver motioned for me to go around where I could sit and ride to wherever I need be going. I came to the back of the truck and discovered a group of well dressed men sitting cross-legged on the metal bed, in the depths of a celebration, a few playing tabla and a string instrument with a gourd base. They passed a chillum and some whiskey. I hopped in and one of the men banged on the wall of the carrier, the truck took off. All of them sat staring at me, laughing. They introduced themselves; they were all lawyers and handed over their cards. They hailed from Haryana a ways southeast and were on their way to the Shiva temple not too far from my house. It was a special time for the Shiva, Shivaratri had just passed. Neelkant road was busy with Pilgrims. They resumed their party. I sang along with them, and smoked and drank. America, they said, "What a funny place. We want to go there, you want to come here. We're switching philosophies for ways of life." We arrived too soon. They said if I ever had any legal trouble in India to call them. They drove off. I wish then to be naked, reading and possibly stoned, but I could not find the correct isle of which I dreamt.

Bhodi was sitting on his bed when I returned, his robe bleached from the sun. He had beside him a jar of kamubucha he had cultivated, and he poured me a glass."You will meet my Guru. We will go towards Mussori." I knew not then in the moment but from our time together that he was a fragile man. My unspoken judgments were of ill comings. I cooked a simple dinner that evening. We sat on the cold floor after the sun had fallen. The food was ill-prepared, double starch. He scolded me for the fact. We slept early, listening to Garcia.

At sunrise. "A walk," said the other. The sun had lined the hills with gold. We walked along the riba. A pool slept beneath a decaying bridge built by the British in times before. Across hid a cave enclosed by large stone made by hands of man. Back, down, and around. We entered the cave to sit. Countless fires had stained the ceiling black. It smelled of original as fragrance came for such a thing. Sitting. A splendid delusion. The mind is quick to do what you wish. We strode back toward the house. "Dreaming Swamis," Bhodi said. "Men who dream the days away." They wake only to become asleep once more. The twirling banyan in that racked-blue wind.

As we crossed the roads of Dehradhun, Bhodi handed me a package from the rear of the cab. I was to deliver said package to his guru. He would not be going with me; their relationship had been compromised due to some recent complications of a social matter. I was dropped at the gates of his guru's home. I stood at a wooden blue gate with mosses. I knocked a twiddle and quickly came a hungry man in a summer blazer and khaki chinos. He greeted me. "Why have you come?"

he asked with a plain face. "I have come to deliver a package to Swami Gjanananda." "Come." He waved his thumb and led me through the garden of flowers. A bench hung down from the floor. "Sit." Near the bench a humming birds stopped around.

Blue-grey eyes and white locks of hair on the old man that walked by. He looked disheveled as Merlin. He looked at me curiously with an aging back and thin spectacles. "You are here to deliver a package to Gjanananda." "I am. The package hails from the States, from some Yogananda disciples. Is here where he resides?""I am he. What is your name?""Prem, I am Prem."I rose and gave him the package. He started for the house and waved for me to follow. A yellow dome topped the house. Inside a grand room with statues of Hindu gods incense burned. Smells of lavender and cinnamon. He motioned for me to sit. A black dog came out from a room, its eyes glazed from cataract. It ran to me madly barking. It stopped at a leg's length and resumed its life. Gjanananda left the room. I sat alone with the barking blind dog. Out from another room an Iranian woman walked, stopping at my side. She paid for the house. She worshipped the man and would let him live there until the end of his life.

He joined us in the room. We sat in a triangle. "Why has this made you come here?" asked Merlin. "To be the courier." "Poor, if that is all," the Iranian woman said. "Yes, I suppose so." "Who gave this to you?" asked Merlin. "Swami Bhodichtananda," I replied. The two of them looked at each other with lowering lips. "What is the matter? "The Iranian woman put her hand on her knees. "He is a troubled man. He has problems with police, and has dealings with the money running. We advise that you to stay away from this man." No difference. "You stay away from him," Gjanananda said sternly. "He is an eccentric man. There may be problems in his character, but what does that mean? We've all run." "Do best for yourself first before the others. "Three men dressed with business strolled into

the room. Each slowly went and prostrated to the man. I bowed
to them. "I recognize you from Rishikesh," one of them said.
"You motor on Neelkant.""Yes, I stay in Ghadughat, I frequent
the town for supplies. Beautiful greens now."
With a titled head the man removed his glasses and cleaned the
lenses. "We are now going to hold a satsang," said one of them.
"It is now time for you to leave.""Yes, that time, thank you."
Scared people, I was the odd man out, the revolving patriot. "Of
course," said the Iranian.She led me out to the gate. The blind
dog madly barked. "Karma," she said. "The dog sees karma in
you. This is why it barks."

Two shitting bulls sat tied to a stake. I walked past to pet
their foreheads. They startled me. Maybe I was bullshit. I walked
down the road to wait for Bhodi. A long while passed and it
seemed too long. The sun went down and the day fermented in
my mind. I thought for a moment that he had left me there in an
act, as if to state, "Now you know my secrets, so I shall be as I
truly am." I waited for a time, enough to sleep a cycle. He pulled
up in the van; we spoke nothing of my meeting.

We came to an empty hotel. The rooms were sprawled
around. A large man with a smoking jacket came out from one
and invited us to join him. The one we had come to meet, sort of
a government official but he also owned the hotels. From what I
could tell, they were discussing the problems and probabilities of
Bhodi owning the land on paper. He would make a trust. The
land was purchased under Bhupi's name. I was tired and dozed
off as I had no interest in finding out the details. We left the
hotel and drove off for Musuri.

Musuri translates to queen of the hills, or, from what the
locals say. Monsurri, the name of a local shrub. After a drive up
through the sky, we arrived at a hotel in a high town. It was an
old British shooting range. It looked out over the land. Old pine
grew up all around. We got a room late and sat in our beds.

Bhodi looked at me. It looked as though he were crying from fighting fear commanded by an abstract conviction, like the Japanese soldier stuck on the island with his musket for fifty years still thinking the war had never ended. We went off to sleep. I lay as a rock under walking trees, I knew very little about these things. I moved slowly and the forces around me scurried and paced. Drooping humans rained as dripping atoms about the land from where I grew. The air slowly sugared until the light came.

A grassy plain looked over nearby lower plains. We did a practice and sat around looking about, at our hands. We demonstrated a few postures to learn. We stayed around the hill some days. It was misty with fog. I walked around near the sharp rock walls bordering the side roads. With nothing black from white to truth and lie I went without judgment. I felt only weight come upon my shoulders when I looked into my eyes. We left.

With two feet I skipped upon return and walked downriver to an opening in the forest across the way. Leaves awaiting fertility covered the floor of the trees with high roots all over. I cleared an area for sitting. The trees spoke not a rude word nor a word at all. The eager sloth comes when all the men go home. He was walking at his dance. Around the forest with the trees standing still, waving silent as the roots below them.

Oh goody wow sir, don't you look rich, so what lessons have
your fingers typed along these gelded reigns?
I'm the smartest in the rooms by tamed and I'd kill us all for the
right amount.
I'd spill our guts and call us trite then gaily gallop all about.
Oh goody wow sir you look rich, so what kind of sounds do your
Grinch hearts shout?
I pay no mind but cannot hear no matter, I removed my ear to
allow her simple voice to loose its nimble clatter.

A handful of mushrooms gets the everything going. The local psilocybin. Hey you, here in the palm now, here is a thought, shhh, it is gone, who am I now? Finis. I walked behind through the trees. Over and around to a new place of trees I had not seen before. There will always be more trees to see. Here now a bird flew to a rock nearby, it danced with its neck smoothly glinting a swirl and slow. Alwry. It exploded with drops of shine. She looked towards me. Wordless, worthless, weightless sky. I swayed back and forth as I stepped on away.

What I claimed to learn is all I have never done. Lightly a little and all that I could. Inhale came and closed your eyes. Goodbye man, constructs man. Material man, the style and rings that rest upon your fingers, these shades that hide the eyes. Your walk of walk prescribed, your arms hang free and have no pockets left to rest. She exploded thy cancerous associations, they rested, exhaled.

Early morning Bhupi rode in on an old CB 720 motorcycle right up to my doorstep. Wherever he went he brought a greasy, cheaply well-dressed worker who stood there with his hands in his pockets, out of place on the land. I sat in my hammock. Bhodi was upstream washing clothes. "Hari om," he yelled over from my door with his teeth red from pan. "Hari om, Bhupi." "Come to check the property with us. Bhodi told me that you are leaving in a few days time. See what is done now, so you can see the progress when you return. "He was a good man, his older brother was his boss. He liked this and afforded him a chill way. The land looked good. The hole for the septic tank was filled with a brick structure to make for the tank. Lines of string lay out marking where the foundation would be. A new trench stretched the length of the property, made for the construction of a new perimeter wall. Bhodi approached as we toured around. "Hari Om, Bhupender G," Bhodi said. "Hari Om," he replied. We stood around. Business. Money. Problems.

Solution. "There seems to be a problem," said Bhupi to
Bhodi."Yes?" "The people of the land say that your land is
actually land belonging to the man across the river. You see,
over the years the river has changed its course. A generation ago
it used to run behind this land. Now it is in front separating it
from across the river." He looked careless. The country. "Old
country shit. This is our land, and the government got that."
"They also say that you are infringing on the property next to
yours with these new lines." "This is my land, Bhupi. No one's
going to fool me out of it. "He disregarded relationships with the
townspeople. He was indifferent. Nothing more was said. Bhupi
went off and we were left to our own devices. Silence. Left out
in that storm.

Yes sir, were young but know of the sun and the rain
but now we say young all of our fun has been slain.
Damn sir, we're old and all we run round for the fame
But now we say old all we see bound is gun bullets rain.

Traverse

Chapter Four

    The third class sleeper car packed full, blue benches worn deep from travelers. The barred windows opened to the air that filled the space with breeze. Across the way Bhodi quietly sat. I read E.M. Foresters *Maurice,* a posthumous work well without its creator. I smiled all the while. It felt good to be going someplace, going someplace simply for the purpose of going some places without preface or race. Eastward locals laughed toward Bhodi, a western man in the orange cloth. He was, but could just as well have been in any other attire. On the bounce he was a white escaped scared, enlisting in yet another prefect's idea of perfect to find home.

    Bhodi and I spoke little of anything really, we'd begin to speak and after not to long we'd realize the comedy in continuing. He shunned what was done before, and what was to come had little to do with what was here now. I did not care for what was said, nor what could have been said if we wished to speak. I might enjoy a century of quips with a good head. But still on the rare occasion we were lent to the lugubrious discussion between us. "You see, you have ended up in this place, in this here way, as you are, pointless to dismount, yes, but in this instance I feel I must know how you have come here. You say nothing of your life and seem to be hardly in favor of it. To me the life stroll may mark the nature of one's being. For some it leads to the end of their lives in white, some falter and abscond to the shadows of black, while others wish only to continue around," Bhodi said, then looked out the window. Always colors.

It was silent. The car was tired just as the clattering tracks, but it always seemed that music was playing. The past was to be of no use to another. The victimization and glorification of the living. I had done more than the last man, therefore I was a better man because of it. To be raised as the hunter of champions. The short. What is one's tall-tale of which he sprawls to remember? I was in my Eden all alone and happy in ignorance to the true shape of things. Taught by ones with lives busy saving themselves, we are only to awaken to the fierce recognition that even the mighty general leading men with guns does not know his next step nor the reasons for his last. The sad old woman screams at the weeds for growing towards the sun. She faces death and has no more tears to shed. To the weeds to let them stand, for what are roses but weeds we have heartily loved?

Bhodi spoke. "Is this not poetics of the escapist, are we not only you, Prem?"I slumber forever regardless of the name. I am because of the way. To become free from what we have become. From around, no matter if we spoke these words presented. The witness to this flowering of a dancing lovely. A young boy came and sat beside us to listen. "You boy, who are you?" asked Bhodi sternly. "I am Sham," he said. He was shy, he was Sham, and he was a child, but he must not have known what he was because he stood for us all. At what age does one experience this questionable existence of the recessed darkness into light, the acknowledgment of this Descartes cliché?

Something to have read. I know only because I do. I resumed the story of my histories. While growing there is only so much one can do with things, so we throw those things out the bus window and make a mess of ourselves red and drooling from laughter. They catch on and recommend that it would be better if we left. "An inciter of riots," they claim. We think that it is a terrible place anyhow; the stiff-lipped feel-good recyclers, the timing speeds of the runners gunning, the running place, the aristocratic neo-Nazis. I had to leave before they got to me, and it seemed by luck it stole me, the fun down yonder. It calls and spits you out in more directions than they knew before they tame the tail to balance. The boy listening had fallen asleep. Fields passed and a man smoked a bidi."I may never know how I grew or how I have come to be," he said. "I was young and simply did not see. Still I do not, but must we know about yesterday to feel good about tomorrow?" A long silence passed as we watched the land.

"Blueberries," Bhodi said, pointing to the passing fields. A few men crouched side-by-side watching the blue land go by. I passed the time by the open door at the end of the car. An elephant passed the tracks. What are flowers worth now to the fragrance of money? I slept in the highest bunk and knew little of the life from dreams. Consumed now by ideas of moving, along with my sleep of dreams. Moving along like I had before in my dreamless wake. Nothing was sacred, and if nothing is, fall away from the others and find freedom in cowering crows up on the lines above. I know but a speck of minutia along the traveled-less's floor, still I think and I think that I want to need more, but know that the ones without heavy heads sickened by these thoughts of the everything and everywhere are for us not to fear but to keep close and around, off the wall and far from the fires.

Those gorgeous, courageous, wandering lovelies. The smile's throne. The newfangled smile. Perhaps I have stared at the wrong wall. Enough. Soon I will be home in this room. The end of this house. These colors shock me. I invite the vibrato.

Varanasi stood before us under the rising sun. The station smelled of wet human and a heavy chutney as we tiredly hailed a rickshaw. It brought us as near to the banks of the Ganges as it could. The buildings so closely nestled, the space between them was far too thin for autos. A cobbled ally led us further into the city, this way and that. A rat ran and the men smoked walking. Mandakini house. We would stay for some time.

The building, as if in suspended animation, stood bare of any modern attributes. Bhodi and I each got a room. I lay in my cot and looked around. This bed and a bathroom with a bucket and faucet for bathing. The chipping walls. Spice. I swayed and had no problem doing nothing. Then as I lounged in a cloud of fame, a loud crash came from above. I wandered up to where Bhodi held his room. He was there, lying in his bed that had collapsed to the floor. He lay sprawled out laughing. "I must be getting fat," he said, and it was because of this way he had to him that I had remained in his company. In this instance it is but a small happening, yet I have met few along my way that see nothing more in the actions of the falling and the rising than simple trivialities far less important than watching that you do not step onto the snails.

The hotel staff came running. They laughed and clapped. One yelled something down the hall. Another man came running with an armful of bricks. Laughter. The hotelmen propped the bed back up level."This has happened before," one of the men said. "The beds are old. Maybe one day we will all sit down for relax and the whole place will fall." His English made his words correct; for him they meant only what they meant. He meant them and did not care.I returned to my room and finished reading *Maurice*. I sat awake on the floor and watched the moon move through the open window. I took a pen to the page for what reason.

Truly, I have made this all for you but I should not show it until I am finished.
This poem I have scribbled since I could not even write seems best before I sleep.
In the night something goes and sometime in the morning it all comes once again.

*Now the poem is not good enough for you nor for I and I write it
once more again.
My friend laughs at my unbinding book still set on the first page
filled up with black.
I laugh and run through the pages, here, they are all ruined by
my shedding eraser.*

A chai walla handed us cups drawn from the clay that
lined the shore. On the banks we watched the river go. Boats
went up and down and up and down. People bathed. It was an
open city. Smoke from burning pyres filled the air. The burning
ghat. We walked over and sat on the steps above. I sat with a
finality the end might bring, as a skull atop the desk of a thinking
man. Bodies burned. We looked on. The men. The costly wood.
The untouchables. The gee and flowers. All easy. The end.
Without the poisoned cookie jar. As commoners we traveled
round with death among us every day. Death quaintly hidden,
only so we did not dispose of our fights for the jagged staged
freedoms. Now we roamed the earth as if we were immortal.
Bravo to the worth of mortality at hand. The humbling flower
fighting the rain even after her last petals had fallen. We left the
ghats and started for the boats to ride the river.

A young rower received us. He dried there in the sun to
support his family. I thought I had done nothing for mine and in
fact nothing for no one not even myself. He got us upriver
through the slow churning current, flowers from prayer floated
by. We parked on the banks opposite the city where the water
birthed a sandy stretch of land that would be covered by
monsoon, but for now it was empty and dry. Bhodi and I walked
along admiring the skyline."You do not seem like you are with
us," Bhodi said, skipping a stone."It seems that way. My mind is
merely taken by the land." The strap of my sandal broke free."I
see," he said uneasily."You seem also like you are not with us," I
said.We kept on.
"The noise and blacking water, people with nonsense in their

heads," he said.

"You know, I feel internally drunk with laughter. We both walk here together, farther from anything we could ever imagine. We are truly wasted." I chuckled.

We stopped and watched the other side, the city.

"One day we will not be wasted, but on this day it will not even matter," he said. These dialogues deceived me. He was modern yet his conservative lifestyle led him to strict interpretations not begetting the ethereal. I could not fathom the idea. For this it seemed that he was judgmental of my persuasions. Curious to know for what reasons I sailed them in my oceans. Silence. I did not want to hear words from a book so I did not confide in him my thoughts then or on many other occasions. Ironically, I read someplace in a good piece of fiction that silence is a terrible thing, thoughts must be spoken or forgotten, and it was thoughts I looked at in the most disagreeable way. I saw only the horizon holding no reservations for arising perceptions.

Rooftops went on and on. Clothes blew with the wind. A man and his son flew a kite together. There were kites all around, a kite from far off cut the string, and they laughed and began fixing another. A girl stood on an adjacent rooftop; she looked with a clear eye. We met with a gaze from a distance. Her face was of a light earth and the golden nosepiece speckled the sun. We looked at one another and youngly laughed. An elder woman came and realized her distraction, and she was tugged by the arm to return indoors.

The sun slowly failed again. I was on the roof alone. Bhodi was in his room. The whole city lived below, I could have known just as much if I were deaf and blind. Then two brightly dressed musicians came, each with a tabla. A teacher and the student. Together they performed some call and response. I listened and removed another tiny piece of worthless wishing contempt from off my young shoulders. The demise of the emulatory. Varanasi would last only for a short while longer. I was sleeping. The burning ghats burned and again the same boatman led us up and down the river. Bhodi and I walked to the water's edge. An overdone prayer. The Brahmans, the poor people covered in shit. Too many people in the show. In a manner ill-inclined to the shape of ritualism like breathing in our sleep.

The peaches' fuzz has bits of dew. Without one step felt, he walks on through; expanse of blue.

I wandered the banks and played out episodes of when I was a child. I was ordered to ingest psychotropic drugs for a period. I knew what they were and what they represented. It was all around. The brain matter. Growing up speaking with highly educated people of the paper class with doctorates and prestigious awards on papers behind glass. The comedy. A child abducting attentive scholars who merely wished to discover his thought process. Just about beyond, merrily waiting. I became so deeply embalmed in thoughts I became entirely unaware and moved along the banks with only my body.

That old man from town came to my door. He wanted nothing. His room billowed with collected droves. Along the plane sweeping up, this room gets grand upon fleeting.

I walked the streets for a lassie nearby. I sat down on the stairs, a bit of hash. The sky reflected in the water, the sky blue, and the sky remained within the river. A boney wayward walking cork of a man wore a glazed-out eggshell dhoti and a black bandanna round his neck. He sat beside me. He looked at me, combing his long grayed hair.
"Imagine boy, the water here, take to remember, if this before you no longer flowed without end. The glaciers meeting the sky, it is only just going to happen. Just as man shall stain the northern ice.""It does not have to be this way," I said.
"And you are here watching us for what? Are you going to save

the world with your thoughts?" He laughed.
" If they ever stain the place, the young would die of unrest, the metals would conquer sure. I don't think paper can save us. It must be something more. An embrace. I guess if I die knowing I've done nothing to imagine the death of such things that we know to be bad in the heart, I shall die a sad and weak man. To produce the embrace, the meek shall inherit the earth. An earth pillaged by the scared.""Ah, you. Bad feelings in the heart, but are they here with us or just feelings void of manifestation?" I left back with more troubles on my mind. Our train for Ranchi was due to arrive. The world was on fire.

He's Walking for words and walking to words.
As he wakes on towards the sun sir I lick and taste these tours adorned.
More walking birds still styling gawking words.
What do you call a writer who talks?
A talker my sir.
Walking grandeur figments of the uppermost echelon, stomping on the sun.
'Tis from the castle of lies where these words do start to pun.
Dungeons in the sky, he writes words until his nails curl and fall from bloodless knobs.
You bastard suits, stooge dames and worthless jobs.
Make your own fuck money run and leave this job to wordless weightless mob.

Ranchi is the name of a bird people of the land consider pious. From the station we take a long ride through a packed fun city of sweat and blood to a grand looking place. High white walls surrounded a compound thick with old trees. A security post let us into lush garden leading to white building. I waited outside as Bhodi went to find us entrance. The grounds were silent. Flowers from each corner of earth bloomed there. The grass was a dark green and looked as if it had been combed. As I waited I stared at my pants. I stood with my hands within my

pockets looking at myself from the eyes. The best pants I ever owned, and they had cost the price of a healthy goat. Bhodi had warned that I should look nice or my welcome might not be offered. Bhodi returned with another monk. He was tall and heavy with a long black ponytail. This was where the bliss came to be ordered and organized. This wealthy place, rich from the pockets of the anxious. "Namaste," he calmly said with wincing eyes."Namaste," I replied.
We were welcomed. Dinner was to be served shortly. We made our way to the room. Fancy rooms. Mosquito nets lay draped over the queen size beds. I lay and read some words on Buddhism and ecology. Still I was robed in my tiny mind and larger fictitious egoic elements. I forgot to remember.

A gathering of people waited outside a dining hall. Monks and disciples of the idle,worshipped, the man they sought to emulate. Bhodi introduced an old friend of his, a tall thin man with black round book glasses. "Nameste, Prem. I have heard that you are a student, trying to find the world in those books of yours." He nodded in acceptance."Yes, it seems that way doesn't it." I put my hands together and raised them, "The rose in a rose bush.""Yes," he laughed, "such beautiful things."We entered the dining hall. Food came round and we ate in silence. I left out alone. A pond rested where giant goldfish swam. We grow as the goldfish grow. We be the everything and every-not but live only when we do. I took a seat on a marble bench beside the pool and looked to the reflection of the moon. A young woman sat beside me. She was brightly dressed and had lost her gaze. Tatiana. "Look there," I said, and pointed to the reflection of the moon on the water."The moon, it is beautiful. I looked at the moon as a girl, and now it is the same moon," she said."Squint. One moon in the water, one moon in the sky, one moon in your mind's view, and one moon in your eye, the fourth reflection." I laughed.She fixed her gaze. Laughter.

I had gone mad and lost the will to speak of passing talk.

I should not kill the fruit before I reap the seeds, I thought. I wished her a sweet dream and returned to my room. Feeling all alone I read a bit of Cummings and felt like a bastard of a writer, to ruin the language. I fell off asleep and a blue woman came to me in my dreams. She gifted me a green box made from a soft wood and ordered that I must not look inside. I walked around the streets of a place that felt like home and never peeked inside. I whistled and sang with the gorgeous all about. Black blue.

Morning bells tolled and the earth came awake for the sun. I bathed. The cold water again. Waking up. Silence. Thoughts. Regression. Hatred. Silence. Bliss. Anticipation. Quarrels. Bliss. Sleep. I made my way down to the main temple lawn. Bhodi was there. All the folks and monks of the place were there on the lawn standing in columns. A high monk stood on the top stairs leading into the temple. I stood with the others. I was awake and ready. Techniques to awakening. Tensing the muscles and breathing in patterns fast and slow. It ended with a prayer and silence and we went on in the temple. A sanskrit statement. We meditated. Meditation. Troubled sharding silence then stillness sharding, the breath running away and then returning. Again, slower and slower. We sat well all the day. Darkness. A surprise. For whatever reason I felt closer to the land.

I left the hall alone and walked through a garden of rose and sunflower. I took to the bench that faced the white marble gazebo in the center of the gardens. Marble screens. Maria sat beside me, just as a bird before flying south. "Here take these keys, Prem," she said in Spanish. "Of course. May I ask why?" I wished for an invitation to her room later in the evening." A monk here, well, can you keep a secret?" "Sure I can." "A Monk here, a tall thin one with big glasses, he told me he knew me in a past life and wanted to meet me in my room. I don't want to cause trouble, and I don't want to be banished from the organization." "I can't tell you what to do, but do whatever makes you feel comfortable." "Yeah, take these keys. I'll meet him, but we can't go into my room if I don't have the keys.""You shouldn't worry. If you want, don't meet with him, stay here with me and watch the land.""I'll go and come back. "The monk she was to meet came into view across the garden. She leapt up and before she left off dropped the keys in my lap. I returned to my room where Bhodi sat writing on his computer, writing a newsletter to Germany. He would be heading there soon to tell some strangers how to live. Up on my bed I took down the words.

The delighted smoking darkens as he sits beneath his chair.
The enticing dark and joking kills his brother while he's bare.
He thinks until he sweats wine red,
He drinks until his mind runs dead.
Another rhyming bullshit as I clasp these laughs beyond.
Another rhyming bullshit as I gasp these breaths I've pawned.

I dozed off but was soon awakened. Bhodi stood at the door. "Prem, wake up, I'm running into town. I will return later this evening. Enjoy the grounds. Use the computer if you'd like, your parents must want to hear from you."

Indeed they were. Alone in the place, there still, I was about ready to run. It all seemed as a worthless joke. Look at all these people dressed in white spitting on the others. And me the escaped. I must be no different than all those parading whites in colors feeding popcorn to the monkeys. I was not the one it seemed and never would be. I had presented myself on my own accord. My father once told me that it was a lie that other people were happy. I saw the Austin Martin with the blond beside the businessman and wondered if he slept well when he arrived home in his palace. I sat ready to drown myself in my own vomit. It is too much to live in this place, I thought. I wished to write my parents and convey that I was fine, fine seeking bliss in the third-world country, learning about all the wonderful things. I wanted to lead them to the lie in which I wished to reside. A bunch of lost people we were and not even in a Hemingway, damn.

I opened the computer to send off a letter. I knew of some pictures taken of the land in Ghadughat, I was in one of them looking happy and well. I wished for my mother to see this picture. I opened a folder on the desktop. I scrolled through and within were large collections of naked young men. My mind arrested and at once I become angry with myself for spending time with Bhodi. I figured it was so. I knew of his sexual persuasions and no care past even simple acknowledgment. I felt more of a human and knew that my own trifles in the search for happiness could be forgiven. The recluse I had become, an angry stupor of contemplative weight free of love and awareness. The monk had never made an advance on me, an awful group of lewd remarks but it was the role he played.. He was a harsh but lovely man. He allowed me to live with him in my cloud. The cliché white led to asking what from freedom by the wacky flamboyant monk. Once more a movement of comedy. To laugh. May we remove   sex   discussion   and   all   other   transgressions, manifestations, and moods of cultural and social expositions from the table, far too simple are these things to be discussed as law, stance, fan, foible, political agenda, or this that and the other. Progress in this short humanity, do as you wish and do not attack, wave smoothly along with without a drop of reaction beneath the black blue. Waste your day and become the superhero. End to the flux paper period.

An associative man ponders sex and may arrive at animal instinct or physiological reform of this that and the other. Acts, ask the animal. We coined him inhumane. The god-fearing man and the animal. Ashamed to be beast and fierce with its movements. Jealous of the rhinos in the field and the mare of the stable. He cries that if he can withstand this animal within him then what is he but a god. Falling to his knees in the face of instinct. Become not a man but the superman upon this tingling orb, the sexy slow stepping, with crown, book, and scepter.

Dinner was served in silence. Afterward outside the hall a man desperately tried to explain to me why the practice of meditation that he used and learned at this place was better than all the rest. What an asshole, I thought. He professed to me that it was a science and that I would only waste my time pursuing any other practice. A fan. The crusaders. I squinted at him. He was a judge himself, the literal, a man who walks the line of balance, swung round. I started towards my room. Maria was there, looking to the petals along the path of white roses. I stood beside her. She was east and her language of movement had already conveyed that she was unscathed by the colors. The monk told her of the past lives they shared, the things they did. He made out to explain in language and understanding the feeling that arose within him when she had showed. The projections of the mind onto words followed by the interpretation of the spoken word for a third round of evaluation. Absolved. He had found her presence so profound in any way that his mind lapsed. She was not the owner of the production. He stood alone to make the show.We strolled around the garden. We shared histories. She loved a man once. He rode horses in the mountains. They went off riding and ate mushrooms in the back hills while congregating with the cows and the crows. One time young Maria punched a boy in the face for trying to kiss her; they called her Ivy from then on just like the character from *Batman*. I met a woman named Maria once and we both lived too fast. I returned the keys, wished her a sweet dream, and returned back to the room.

I did not confront Bhodi. I instead broke my promise to Maria and asked him what he thought about the incident of which I had been partly involved. He thought it ugly. The corporation would not stand for such a thing to be raised across the tongue. He was then fighting himself, for he knew himself to be aflame. The struggling monk. All of our internal dramatics.

To what did I owe myself the pleasure of attempting to cross. Hypocrisy. Not another animal can produce such a device. I sat uneasy that a journey was forever scathed. We spent few days more, each in meditation. Silence. Unrest. Death. Awake. The birthday of Yukteshwar, an old-day ascetic. An eagle of a man. The rested. His picture presented me with another idea to face. I wished for his company, I wished to find an idea of mine like him to sit and speak of the simple things. Our own color blue. Warhol's can of soup in another era. I gave my farewell to Maria with a hug and she whispered that I be as wonderful as I could imagine. We hailed a rickshaw outside the compound walls. City streets lined with garbage, the traffic ringing, and the people running and yelling. A catch of a place. We rode off to Puri.

Jaganath Puri was an ancient place. Cashew trees grew right up to the beach to meet pine. An easygoing healthy monk opened a blue gate and invited us in. It looked as if the vast property was free from residence. A collection of buildings with small rooms for sleeping and a few temples were around. I lay awake in my bed below a mosquito net. I listened to the sounds of the woods around us. They were wet and the coast was close, the air was moist and the breeze warm. I drifted off. I awoke alone and wandered out. I walked along the empty open building. Characters of an alphabet I could not recognize took up a board in thick white chalk outside the large temple across the room. I walked up a flight of stairs, wooden French doors dark heavy with rain led into a dark hall. Bhodi and others sat perfectly still maintaining lotus. Silence. With eyes shut they breathed in quick successions. I joined them sitting on their ground, then above in my plain of shows. The breaths. I tried to forget about bliss.

Literatures polluted my mind. From simplicity to the ultimate complexity, cellular, ethereal, other. Words on the evolution of consciousness from the perspective of a trans-personal physiologist. The evolution of mankind, his civilizations, and the evolution of the human consciousness. Our first visions of God, interpretations of the sun becoming mother. Becoming modern Catholicism, industrial revolution, all of this. Perceptions of the same. I did not know that I knew. My own woes were of no consequence, not to the future of mankind or to the evolution of consciousness. I had nothing to say, thinking too much. Life was the old painting whitewashed back to canvas. I could see nothing from a man and nothing of a man. No structure of a working place, no smoking from a project, just there the fresh air of salt, pine, and musky smells of sand. The senses held no weight. We were the witness to the will of the others, and the others, the will of the amorphous.

I lay awake in bed salty from the sea. I lay awake troubled with menial hypocrisies. What we do but never think. What we conjure yet never do or make. Our thoughts; the amorous myriad creatures of the seasons playing games of the king. My subconscious politics of the protective egos. I played over songs of Kumar Gondharva to find sleep. Tomorrow we would travel to Bhodgaya, the sitting place of Buddha.

Four red-robed monks round a table watched a tube television eating thenthuck. Each of them smiled with dimpled faces. Bhodi and I sat at across from them. It was dark and the restaurant was three mud walls with a low cloth roof."The bodhi tree is here," Bhodi said. I knew it from a book. "Still gonna return west?" he asked.
The West was on my mind. New York City. Family love. Fun night friendships. Summers on the run.
"I feel like I've got to go back to play in this place," I said. Although the whole of my anticipations had escaped me, my dream had yet to pass. "If I don't do what I feel I can't imagine that I'll ever be able to relax here. Funny, here I can, now I can, and here I cannot, of course. I have a twirling in my stomach. I must produce the heavy feeling about my body in the others. Something so true and clear to another they gasp and feel as if it

were their own. To be wild and vomit upon the stage. To shit
under the chairs."
"Yes, thank you," he said and nodded with a smile. "Everybody
wants to go kill something inside of them so they feel better.
Then you can come back, defeated or completed. If you can say
that, you'll be back."

All in. All in-scape, stone. Vincent van Gogh painted
himself as a Japanese monk. He wrote, "A simple worshipper of
the eternal Buddha." One man looks at the sky and sees it,
another looks to feel a movement. Both are none the wiser. The
war without command. We finished our tea and started back to
our room. We'd gotten a room in a monastery. As I lay awake
under the buzzing mosquito net, music touched my ears. Close
by from the porch, lights lit a portion of low clouds in the sky. A
wedding was celebrated on the land behind the walls around the
room. Bhodi was frustrated with the noise. He tossed around and
covered his head with a pillow as a moody hermit might. I left
out to see and gather water. I snuck up and sat on the back wall
surrounding the place. I tore a piece of cloth from my large
apron of a shirt and tied it around my wrist. I entered the back of
the wedding and lost my concern for water. Crowds of people
danced. A wedding of wealthy families. I quietly sat at a table
looking over the party. An elderly women put her hand on my
shoulder. "They just met each other not one year ago," she said.
"The bride and the groom. Some say that arranged marriage is a
whole ruckus but I say that marriage is a team, love comes
naturally to all who realize their own possession. We can love
anybody. Why not let your team decide your next mate?" She
had never worked a day in her life and had that easy smile a life
of relaxation may afford. "One day you too will get married, and
what a lucky girl. Children. Oh how I love the children."

I guess I too must travel the road, I thought. A whole
story, a whole lifelong epic of a story. I got so fucked up

thinking how abundant these outlandish possibilities were, the imagination endless and from a place void of color. I snuck back over the wall and slept lost in dream, wondering which life I would like to have till sunrise.

Beneath the bodhi tree. The marble floor. Meditation. Buddha sat here, I thought to myself. To think to meet him would disturb the notion to be him, but for what are we here? To desire to be remembered of the Buddha? Had I lost the understanding or was it never mine to lose. Why have I come here from so far to sit? Silence. I had been sitting a lot in India, and most of my time spent there my eyes were closed. A leaf fell from one of the branches into my lap, and I carefully slipped it into my pocket. There were many other people and many more leaves but they were not important. Walking the grounds I watched the monks prostrate to their Divine on wooden platforms worn from prayer.

Bhodi ordered a cucumber and tomato salad in an open cafe. I sipped a ginger lemon honey tea. With my tea I walked into the tailor's beside the stall. An excited man greeted me and immediately began measuring my every bit. A good price, so I got myself a set of white linens made to fit. I asked for a few custom pockets with Velcro. The clothes would be ready the next day. I went back to where the German that Bhodi had mentioned was present. "Hari om, Prem G," he said "Hari om."A fair amount of things were spoken about, drab detail of terrible things. It was a shame. The German was a loud man who had no idea of the mess that he was making in the air around him. He invited us to view the progress on his projects. I said nothing. In the rickshaw the German attempted to create witty quips directed towards our uneducated driver. He is sad. I am sad, too, I thought. I wondered how I was to love these people.

Through the small villages near the outskirts of town we came to a soft yellow building. Flooded rice fields were all around. Smoke from mud huts covered the air, and some small children ran past us as we entered the place. We walked the dark stairs to an open, double-level roof. I left Bhodi and the German behind and ascended to the second level. A sun shined man was standing in the corning beside the railing. He wore layers and layers of shirts and looked out of place in the hot sun. I approached and he gave a wince of his eyes. He wore the layers to save energy. It was energy he was after, the Qi, the prana, the energia, elan vital. He was as a sponge to the air as he looked to the sky. As if the breath is a state of mind that may end if we willfully accept our being is saturated in this atmosphere of which we are, only physiologically removed.

The slow breathing sun shined moved all at once. He was satisfied, I be with him for forgetful moments. A Japanese shows. He had come to live in the company of this man, to emulate. The disciple. I could not dare to explain how these people were, what we spoke or what we radiated. The most interesting person to me has nothing to say. What a trip of silence, fortified by the echo by relation by comprehension and of man.

The joker makes me smile before he delivers a joke because I know that he is a funny man. I attempt words for one but fail; it is the fault of the language we hold. We shall struggle through terrible mires of words. The sad master cannot write the truths of reality, he may only experience them in hope to seed his friends. Yet somehow, in this there are these lines and paints that have produced no show but simply deduce you to the subject of beauty of which you never saught. I live with you only for this. I have tasted and now I am awed. The cacoethes pallet.

We rode off to the cave of Gautama. Sandy plains. A rough ride along the trails. We took shade and rested below a Bodhi tree, the same species Buddha used. The roots of it stem from the branches and travel down into the ground. I climbed up its arms and found a chair in its palm. In the distance across a dry river lay high hills of peach stone. I want to buy a piece of land here I thought. A school for children. A farm and well-read teachers. A positive future led by the proudless, braveless lovers. Just a dream. I am poor and stupid, I thought, I should run back west and race and race until I can create the dream we live within.

We rode on past half-built abandoned temples. Warm breezes. We left the bikes and walked though a herd of baby goats blocking the small path we had followed in. The houses around were mud, sheet metal covered with palm leaves. Naked children followed us laughing and amused, they whistled and spun. Some women harvested a red fruit from the trees. One approached and offered some. Delicious, a cherry of a fruit. We remounted the bikes and kept on. When we came to the hills and the bikes could go no further, we started up the road for the cave on foot.

The cave blackened by the fire has too much show. It was perfectly shaped inside as if it had been carved by a sculptor. A spot overused. I had no interest in it and left immediately after I had entered. I wandered over to a ridge and saw a stone archway in the distance. I started for it. "Off so soon?" Bhodi yelled." Over to that arch." I responded without a care or glance. Sprawled out flat land lay beyond the hanging arch of the peach stone. A cliff went straight to the ground. It was windy, and the wind through the arch made a light whistle. The rumble from a hive hanging nearby made the hill hum. Bhodi joined. "We do all of this to be grounded and then we see the ground is up," Bhodi laughed.I went off in my mind and saw a Chilean scene:

We walk along the high plains beneath the crumbling mountains. A river runs out from the ground to a pool from which a stream flows east and another west. Old time ice-water lays round glacial shadow. The land quickly ascends around. Arctic grass circles with sharp green blades stay still in the wind.

Gonzo leads us with a hopscotch into the Andes. Dave is there, Gonzo's wife at the back. We walk up on the flat before the end of the dyeing volcan sufre. The top view leads to the ranges out far till the curving earth hides them. Argentinian peaks sharp like knives and of a different color than those to the west. Below perfected blue water collects in the bosoms of earth's upward punches. To drink the view. We jump to the wind and it gives a fight. We look on when the stars show their light that travels still, after they're dead and gone, the day that never was. Dave and I look to the sky and know nothing of what we sew, it is the beauty given, he and I never expect anything less. Enchantment alive while the imagination runs away from the old teacher discarding fake words discovered by the children.

The air went warm through my hair as we passed through India, the streets of Bhiar.

Take my hand and I will dance so that the leaves are fell in pairs

You pile them and jump in them often blissful and bare.

Oh don't pose your fake doze, off gone to stare.

Take my hand in the leaves frightful pile.
As to smell these last leaves and walk in them for a while.

Round

Chapter Five

I returned, and that square house across the river was waiting where I left it. My hammock hung blanketed in leaves dried by sun and the Riba ran low from dehydration. The world called while I was out. Over in town I looked at my neglected social networks and called my parents. They were concerned that I might be losing my mind to unsound theories of life, incompatible with those of the Western man. My friends had given up on wondering what happened to me. I was not concerned. I told them what I thought all parents and friends must hear, that I was fine, doing different healthy things, that my face was still intact and that I would one day return and all would be well, and that maybe the only difference in me would be my skin stained well from the sun.

No place to run; to be on the run.
take breath.
beyond the fearlessness of death.
What you have is yours and just enough for all.
More is nothing to stop you and less is still to call,
It's no longer now a picture round to go in lives of knowing.
The open door to the shed of my tears in these days that we'll be going.

I reserved myself a place at a school of yoga down south and could go if I chose. Change was calling, Bhodi was driving me to a place of anger and the more reactions I witnessed the further enraged I became within. Mohan told me about it; he was a good man, his advice would also be good. Bhodi went to the same school long before when he had first moved to India. It was a different time then, it was more difficult to get here. He said that now it would be what I expected it to be. The magazine. A change of scene, I thought, I'll go mad if I stay here killing my characters. Reigns blew to the wind. To return back to the land I had only to walk through town. Something of an agoraphobic

I must be, I thought. I must have receded to far within without the heart, the public begat me to shudder. Clouds of projection; bodies styled. It was me and it was them. The world had come to this place far into the mountains. The Beatles came here and flew around in a helicopter; it was a tour of a town. It was everywhere and I was more alone with no place left to run. Stalemating my head to head south, I cleared the earth in a corner of the land where growth had come back. I tilled some soil and made way for some seed. We set a hose to siphon the water from the canals above the property. The foundation of a double room was set in place. Work went steadily and I watched Bhagat smoke his chillum in the mornings by the river. I joined him often with a mango and some free pages for my hand.

The stance you pose implies that you care for nothing in this place.
Your calloused palms and daylight lies say different just in case.
Agree the butcher of the killers are most hated in the town,
agree that he's the best fed with a lawn strewn with rusty plows.
Torn jeans, tobacco and drinking after work;
worn dreams, macho, thinkings never worked.
He kept the letter in the draw to walk without his gun.
He is none the better in the maw now chalked with rum.
Dressed in white afraid to scribble,
he's drunk too much and now he dribbles.
Brother the boat left yesterday and you have not even packed,
Life has come and gone today and has left only this knick-knack;
A jewel to wear and then to smoke the point of which they wish to
smite.

A silly little bunch of words that we now speak together: a lily's little
trunk of birds we let fly free forever.

I sat with a tea and watched the flies and old men of the town who had lost their minds long before. One walked the fields at night looking for his wife. She left him for another man when his hair was still golden brown. Sitender strolled in. He had brokered a deal of corn and wore a new pair of boots. The country had stolen him. At tea time words were sparse. The dark little stall below the road line gave shade and soft music. Nothing went on. A seasoned Swiss man walked in. He always yelled in town but today he was quiet. Sitender left. To the life colored black and white, what was important to my pocket empty of money? What was my pocket worth to this Swiss man? He invited me back to his home for more tea and crackers. We stood on his open roof overlooking the town. He lived along the bend that crossed the trickling falls. He was rusty and wore cloth wrapped round his head. The couple of times I was over there, sick sadhus lay moaning around, wounded soldiers of mental freedom. He ran a free clinic. It all felt very pointless. Repetition. Silence. Between positive and negative rests the cacophonous life.

With all the world to think about, through imagining the ultimate complexity, I had tricked my mind into thinking that I could conceptualize even a morsel of this. I kept on with the doings I thought best to be doing, as if there were somewhere to go and things to be done. I woke at dawn and ran through the hills. I passed children on their way to school and they yelled and ran after me. I came back and did slow movements along the river and some silent sitting on the water-chilled pebbles. I went on through these motions absentminded. I stared at a white dot on a boulder until my eyes teared up, until the boulder disappeared. I read all that I got my hands on and the more I read the more disenchanted I became with mentalities, the races, I did not want to race, as if there are others to race. I had no game to myself and looked to others as reference, the models. I am the model and I must know this but I falter in my stance beside my silent friend when she answers me not when I call but only when I do not.

These silly ideas of paradigm.
I drink them still but smile
An order of letters upon the shelve of wild without one sold
These silly ideas of place and time
I think them still but smile
An order of letters beyond the help of any old idiots rhyme

Those barbaric implementations of intellectualism by way of instinctive choices. Bang. To disregard our animal and act on behalf of the true self, beyond the crayons of the intellect, the point of reference. The absent desires to fulfill compassion. The eyes refuse to accept her body. We part and parcel to infinite commodities, selling money yet again for the fifth time. We sit picking our toes. I ramble, frustrated in hopes to achieve more from life; damn it, enough of this. Enough of these systems and itemization. My practice grew slow and became something I did only for escape, finding comfort for bliss, bliss in motion. I could not find friendship with any stagnant bliss.

I would head south with these ideas from a morbid place. Along with myself, Bhodi had grown strange. I saw in him my own dejections of peace. He was always Bhodi. Just as I, his eyes moved faster as he lost time. I am but a changeling scrounging for an anchor in the windy life. We went on and watched the work. The work was slow and for each step forward achieved, a half step back followed. The townspeople soured as the days came in hotter and hotter. They walked and talked with a negative sentiment towards the whites dancing about their forefathers' land. Bhodi chose to build his home before the temple structure, and this was not how it was done in the country. Besides, Bhodi didn't treat them right. He acted more important than the townspeople. Maybe it was the mission he imagined himself to be involved with that brought him to this mood, the crusader. Still the ownership of the land was debated. One morning on the stairs with a spliff I watched the house across the river succumb to the flame, the baths of whiskey generated a great color and wind blew the fire to a great roar. The plans for Bhodi's house proved more difficult than expected. The first walls were torn down due to insufficient design, the mood was cordovan if it had a color, Bhodi was nothing good for company. Somehow in his attempt to organize on paper how to tell people a better way of life he became fully consumed with the politics of religion and spoke ill of most things. Our communication dwindled to an even lesser place in the days before I left; he wore the face of contempt and walked with a spacious arrogance, he began to treat me as an inferior no matter the deed or jump I took.

Early morning I walked to the spot I cleared in the forest and thought of delusion. Another time there and still I was the same. I sat there small as I am below the tress. Before I could make any sense of things my body got up rapidly and kicked around leaves on the forest floor. I cursed myself and started for the confluence downstream. A peacock drank. Down a bit further women stood in the current washing clothes against the rocks. The Riba met the Ganga across from an old empty looking ascetic compound. A sheer wall of loose stone rose, leading up to a ridge that went back up along the Ganga. I started up it, stones fell into the water below. I feared for my life only to reach the top unsatisfyingly alive. I sat between two trees. The wind blew. A herdsman walked easily along a goat path a ways below. Why was I leaving? I spoke with all my millions of characters. I must. A few demanded that I must see more. Some others demanded. Maybe I knew too much, a couple said. Yes , I know too much, one said. Thoughts of a wasted mind hurtling to be loved. Off I was.

The ride to Kerala went. Bhodi told me not to lose my mind. He said that if I left I would not feel free when I returned, my mind would be polluted with the world. I have betrayed myself, I thought. I'm going to spend a month in a magazine ashram with Westerners who wanted to experience India by paying for it. What a moron. A break maybe? I wanted this for some reason or else I would not be doing it. I wanted sex. Women robed my mind. I am no perfect bloom, I am as the flower who wished for water too often even when the rain was falling.

Two Muslim men sat on a bench across from me. I sat by the open bared window. We were in the third class sleeper car. These guys told me they had just worked thirty days on an oil rig, now they had thirty days off and were heading home. They claimed to have loved their jobs but missed their family. A Hindu student of engineering sat beside me, an old man from Iceland, a banker, sat beside him. Moving along the tracks we all spoke something. "Life is nothing more than a succession of perceptions, the world never changes, only the way we see it. Tomorrow I shall not be who I am and was today just before who I am no longer," said the man from Iceland with a smile. "I work and that's about it. I get women, I get love, I give women love and friends friendship." He took a drink from a flask he removed from the inside of his grey suit jacket. "Fuck it, man. We work thirty days on, thirty days off. We get to see real well the reason for all this shit. It's all addiction, just find one and ride with it. My friend smoked like a train on land, but he's not allowed to smoke on the rig. He got so desperate once he started to chew the tobacco from a cigarette. You should see him when he gets off. Life is a succession, pleasure and then loss." What a life in everyone. The train was a real home to diversity. There were no judgments in the land of compromise.

On these trains I encountered more people free from avarice than I passed in the golden streets of New York. Perhaps that was why they all look to the floor. I could not breathe when I saw this, the fate of the modern man. We do not stop to think about the bloom, I thought. How can more be witness to the bloom? Is it so beautiful the fearful rage with anger and hatred upon its exposé? Is this why they killed Ghandi? I could return home knowing that I am a fool. I could return not to be happy or sad, only be and be satisfied and my fate should grow well from there. I am unique but must accept our hearts to be the same. This is crazy. I want to help but know I cannot change the world. Why I ask, who is to be the one? Where is superman? That evening I washed myself with a bucket of cold water in the train bathroom before going to sleep. I slept in the top bunk and wrapped a dhoti around some shirts to make a pillow. It was warm enough to sleep without blankets.

The rain came down hard. Crowds packed nose-close gathered below the bus station over hang. It all smelled of manure and gasoline. I boarded a bus. Stood. The bus stopped in an empty place. I hailed a rickshaw. It was in the middle of the night. I got dropped at the gate of a compound bordered in a maroon wall. I was met by foreigners. I signed some papers. The staff directed me to a dormitory where my bed was located. I fell asleep to sounds of the lions roar.

I do not want to bore myself by storytelling of the worldly people who had escaped their illusions, but were just as I. We awoke at sunrise and did an hour of sitting, together like a herd of helpless goats. We did an asan practice together like useless monkeys sick with humor. We took lunch. We worked around the compound lawns, together like Huxleys hunting worms. A daily lecture on the aspects of yoga and its philosophy. The monk that ran the place was a clean man, truly introspective and humble, too. He was once a doctor in south Africa where he was born and raised. I asked only one question the first day and none after that. "What do you think about the evolution of consciousness," I asked, "in terms of, do you think that we as animals were always awake to our true self or are only becoming so as we evolve much like organic evolution?" A dumb and pointless question my ego told me to ask. "What do you think?" he responded. More questions come from questions, go and ask them of the ethereal. Edison asked too many questions in class so they asked him to leave. After our class we did another asan practice. With the time allotted for rest I smoked joints in the brush. We took dinner. Before sleep we chanted and sat in silence without a word. Hums in the jungle, a warm and happy place. It was all again like blind pigs. Missing perfect by way of thought. I wrote.

The boy bites snakes and he's been poisoned.
His poignant plunders pass below his bright black blue horizon.
His swollen hands hold steady loading guns that we rely on
anointed by the brush of color that is set to swim for eons

I walked out from morning meditation. The first one to leave. Most stayed behind and spoke to one another about this hallucination or that. I walked near the temple where prayer is spoken. Three women. So beautiful the women. I felt that they had stolen my mind to the uppermost degree. I said man, I could never talk and only stare and my eyes would say nothing bad. They came and joined my company. One was from Germany, one from Australia, the other from Ireland. "The whole of the place is going to the beach together. We were going to go alone, take the train home, go for the day," one said. I did not know what I sought so I agreed. We hailed a rickshaw outside the gates. The three of them had been there a few days longer than I and were getting restless. They lit up as we motored off. A bus took us the rest of the way.

Each girl was different but neither knew what they were doing. We knew only that we wanted to leave and most appropriately spend time at the beach. We took lunch near the station, then began asking around for good piece of empty sand. An old seek over heard my questions and recommended we go to a beach by the name of Q. A rickshaw driver got us there. It was a long way, we smoked all the while. He would wait the day for our return. Through young growth and hills of dried red mud, a perfect stretch appeared before us. Coral was right off the break. The water was blue and the sand white. Palm trees lined the back. We swam as children in the waves. I left the girls swimming and walked on a ways down the beach to a small peninsula. I disappeared around the bend.

A cement house went right up to the beach. A lanky woman with long white hair and bandit blue eyes called me over from the porch. She was a Westerner. She must have been left here from the sixties when the Goa scene was going well, I thought to myself as I walked towards her. She stood at the end of the porch. I took a seat in the sand. "One hundred and eighty degrees of nothing you see!" she said, smiling and spreading her arms. "Ain't no place else can we find this." She removed a fly from her tea and went on to take another sip."Only the Arctic's down there," she said. "Clarity for a long ways." She shuffled inside and returned with a jar of water. She walked to the sand and handed me the glass."In 2012, the world is going to catch fire, boy. Everyone will run to the water, but I will already be here.""The world is going to catch fire?" I smirked. "Is the world not on fire now?""Yes, well, you see alright, but you'll see still. But don't worry, you'll be fine. Why are you here, anyway?""Living as much as I can," I laughed."Ah, I see," said the woman. " It's a never ending journey towards the end of nothing and once you reach the end the beginning comes again. Why take classes when there is no god damn test?" I laughed. "It's true, sweet mangoes waiting to fall." We both laughed. "Fuck, if only we could be a little more naked and a bit more stoned all those suits wouldn't be so angry with soft cocks," she said. Then she threw her tea in the air. "I wrote a poem like that the other day," I said. "Sex and stonings, huh, that simple. It's so simple either which way it's nearly impossible to comprehend. Fuck." She came closer and said, "In fact, we cannot comprehend a thing. It is so simple there is no comprehension. Comprehend that."

I don't know if that woman really existed, she probably did, but it's just as well she did not, some other things were said, much better things that I cannot recall, they're on the tip of my tongue really, but so far away. She told me I could come back any time and live there if I liked. I walked back around the bend where I had left the girls. I told them nothing of the gray woman. The German was without a top and her breasts were free in the sun. The four of us sat with a chillum living as far from the obsequious conformist as I imagined possible, just around the bend. I took to the page as we said nothing till the sunset came and finished.

The Dorian deploys his games of sight and wishes that we see,
the doubling back on fake ignored and winded epiphanies.
I sell my words on down the river with two pennies on one eye.

See that luck denies you entrance in the games you need escape.
Breathe all those snuck little kisses you've embroidered on your cape
I sell my words on down the river with two pennies on one eye.

I am here friend, I am here. Catch me as we die.

About time to head back towards the ashram, we got one last meal out on the town away from the magazine. We drove back towards the main strip to a good place by the water. We ate and drank like kings facing a death sentence the following day. We ate for so long, by the time we were finished and back on the streets the last bus had come and gone. Laughter. We went on to another bar and continued to drink. More drinking, more confusion. We stumbled out of the dark smoky place and found a hostel. By way of singing Sanskrit song about love and liberation the hotel clerk allowed us all to share a room. "Most unorthodox," he said. We slept well in one bed. The German wore nothing. We spoke lightly into the night. We returned to the place we paid for. Across the lake roamed captive lions for tourists to come and gawk at. Their cries for freedom horrified me in the night. If I were a bigger man I would have gone and helped them escape but I am no such man, the liberator of lions, imagine. Crocodiles swam, and we swam anyway. The daily routine kept its way as it does and we disappeared. For smoking company I had a good man from England, a hippie chiropractor with a rare vocabulary. We spoke late into the nights, us and an Indian son of a rich man. We laughed over the nature and perception and remedial aspects of civil life. The Indian was due to become a lawyer, the Englishman was supposed to be a doctor. "We've escaped, we've escaped the complex thoughts, and we've escaped what we've made messy of our selves. We've escaped," we said, "from the stars we have." More smokes towards delirium. A pen back in bed.

Here she writes of silence and the scholars curse and groan.
There she writes of valiance turning tailored ghosts to gold.
The foiled repetitions of these words we've got to know.
Dare see fights of silence and our friend shall see you home.

The course neared its end and people got sad, sad to leave each other and sad to leave the magazine, sad to leave with the state of mind they had forgotten to destroy. I sat in the cafe with my English friend; we had just gone for a swim. He thought his life was over. He did not want to return to his job, his unhappy girlfriend or his shitty brown house in the business district. I felt for him. What a poor English man. Two pretty women sat at our table. We cheered up. Achara and Carla. Although Achara was raised by Germans in Germany, they had adopted her from Thailand when she was still a baby. She spoke not a word of her home tongue but a well rounded English and German. She was city cut but country bred, a strikingly original way was to her. I wanted her. When we caught eyes we would not look away, only smile in mutual agreement that the world is indeed too fast for people like us, for us all. My mind seemed unable to be stolen by a woman and hers a man. Bitter confusion had taken their places. I paid little attention to her friend Carla. She had an anger and pride about her person. "We're going to get a houseboat in the backwaters. You should come with us," Carla told me. Of course. She was nice now.

Sad indeed to speak a note strung, but sad, could the word have any resonance? I am no good for the goodbye, I like to think that I like to continue on, but as I do, I feel more fully. A wish. To continue from place to place and thing to thing without a break in end or start, if I return or see you once more it shall be as it was, nothing less and nothing more, maybe more if we are lucky. To replace the sad I should use nothing at all. It simply was, to leave such a wonderful place. The place I ridiculed before I arrived, while I was there, and after I left. It was suffering I was after and it did not live there. If only you could write a book of silence. I could not do it here in this land of clean and ordered silence. The rules destroy. Curfew and Westerners everywhere doing this that and the other from healthy bound books with shiny blues and expensive yoga mats. I was out of place, and felt somewhat stupid for leaving my country abode. At least I had spent a good time sitting, but there would always be more sitting. Fuck, I think. Veritable eternities inside and above it and still my eyes were closed. What good is epiphany in the dark?

And it was I who came from this thought, as if I were alone, as if not all young men dream of a better world. As if a ways down the river we all shall reveal our true fear of those who now sit in the dark room waiting to give advice to the next mind that stumbles through the gates.

I sat on the bow below a green canopy watching the water go. Achara and Carla lay asleep across from me. I looked to Carla and saw with judgment that she was the maternal type. A self-proclaimed yoga instructor out of Brazil. The yoga of exercise some liked to associate with asan. She was middle-aged and well groomed from being married to a wealthy man. In her time in India she had cursed her life and fallen in love with a Monk of the magazine compound and could not call herself good for having sexual feeling towards such a person. She could not believe her inner tendencies and resolved to donate a good rest of the year helping poor children. She was lost in her perception of things. To know everything and then nothing. Oops. You could see it in the way she answered the simple questions, as if she had to think about her own name. I looked at Achara. Both were perfect in the sun. I was lost as they were but I was at least floating around paradise with these hard-to-find people. Achara, she was the young independent, she wanted it all and wanted it done by herself alone. But like all who wish to swim without clothes she had quit her high-level job out of Munich to come check out the yogic life. Lost, what was true and what was false after being in the play of madness for so long without even realizing? Initially she came in search of a boyfriend that left the city for the aesthetic life. When she found him, he was far too involved in the corporations of spirituality. She stayed to find how a way of life could be more enticing than herself.

Long canals lined with palm-covered islands. Three men worked the boat; they were sick with happy and doe-eyed, contagious. I stared at the water and then the day was over. We unloaded to an ice cream shop in the middle of nowhere, like the mirage of soda in the dessert. We sat and ate watching out over the water. I took a pen.

The heating skins feel to find this vessel all within the clay stack.
The fleeting pleasures sung best blind lay nestled in the stray black.
Beating faster coming harder one more time we come together.
Over there, do not mind or bother.
Pastors meeting humming father once again spake no forever.

We docked at another island. A village missed by Westerners since the seventies. Quite easily bullshit, a lie to lubricate the wallet, but still the idea seemed good and again made me feel as if I were doing something relevant. We docked beside a small strip of land with a path going into collections of old growth. A dreary looking village showed from out the brush. We walked by the homes of grass and leaf. Townsmen and women emerged. They followed us along. The younger children had never seen whites from the West, they tugged on my sleeves and poked me as I walked on. They did not ask for money, they wanted only my attention. They did their best interpretations of the West. A cunning fat man with a red ponytail stood in the road before us; he was the voice of the village.

"Namaste," he said. We bowed and gave him our attendance.

The man scurried off and entered his home beside the path but quickly emerged with his wife who carried a plate of teas. "You must help the planet," he said, passing around the tea. "That is your only responsibility." An enormous thing to say in the deep of noplace. "All you city people don't understand the power you have, the affluent, you're busy crying over spilled milks and delving into the terrors of your own dramatics and you forget about the men of the country, the children of the country and the women, the country itself. From where you came, you'll cover this place in cement before you all start to cry for one another."

We sat on logs beside the path and sipped the tea. Although they knew of our world and all its gold and shit, the village was silent. Effectually, news did not exist there, for it did not color them. Politics had no place there for they grew to get along through ways of discussion. It seemed unscathed by the complex inventions of the modern mind, the miles of slandering poetic law for us to misinterpret in a day more once the language morphs. The lost acronyms. "Be that as it may, but it means what I think it does," said the man who hid behind his desk.

The trees and the water, the way they look together, green and blue, sometimes very nice in the rain. They have not changed yet we call the contemporaneous progressive as if modernity implies change. We are the modern man and we are steadfast in our stance for peace and serenity. There are no passive assassins, only the rose petals fall; the thorns remain even after the last colors have fallen.

The country man gave me a bottle of toddy to enjoy when the night came around, an alcohol procured from the local palms. He though it lucky to share the company of two young women and pinched my ass as I left. The children walked us back through the path and returned us to the boat. "Thank you," they said, and smiled and danced. That evening for the last hurrah the chef prepared a special dinner. We ate below the canopy in the low bow and drank a bit of the toddy. Sad for the world, I concluded that a truly compassionate man must cry at every turn but I was not he. May I create the passive assassin from the palace of the sundance. I was bitter and on the edge again of wanting to leave this place. Women always made me feel more whole, more important. A whole lot of nothin'. I offered Achara a space in my bed that evening with a mention that it would be nice to speak with her. I sat out alone on the bow looking to the darkened waters.

Gallantly stand before them and do not fear a morsel.
Patiently brand and deplore them to be dear and simply cordial
To be here. Without wise. Without wit nor one surprised.

Fuck

The moment is wrecked now that I've tried on her disguise.

I joined her a bit after she had gone for rest. Silently in the dark I went beside her and pressed her hand, we kissed and slowly found our way into one another. We floated around canals with the noise. The breath and pleasure of another around me and the tingling shakes of this uncontrollable body fighting for embrace.

Next morning we lay together watching the waters through the bay windows. We headed back to the compound to stay a night. I would fly north and tour some places with Achara; she would fund my travels. I was heading up anyhow, I thought, and had to return to Rishikesh. What the fuck was that place? I wondered. We went along.

A Matisse painting titled The Boat hung upside down in a museum one time for over three months and not one of the visitors noticed. The airport, after being removed from these moments of invention, for even a short while, was a dry and faceless place. All the people so well dressed, floors polished and waxed, everything and one proving something or other. It was a period of self-loathing because I was the world. The trip was short, the airport of Delhi, enormous plastics. We found a hotel for the night. Achara had money and was accustomed to luxury. Flat-screen televisions and silk sheets. I stood in the shower singing. It was the first hot shower I had taken since my arrival. Her head tilted up and her legs crossed at their center. A smile longed to be released but the timid nature of her expositions restricted her from doing so fully without remorse. The moisture in her eyes was quickly laughed away before it had even the slightest chance to mature into a tear. She lay for consumption across the bed. A simple threaded black slip gently hid her. She read a sutra. With my hand I drew shallow dipping circles at her hips and up below her breasts. Her eyes closed and gave into tempestuous movement. From her center, into her. We swayed and sweltered in the heats we slowly served. Every bit of her trembled as we came together in clean breaths. Stripped bodies wet with a lust that did not leave. We thought nothing of it and fell asleep in the city.

An embrace of fainting flows blowing outward on below
I take her down to where this heat escapes above the molding colds
Gasping on and gone beside before we left the novas hide
We dare continue boldly branding tired strewn out done complied
In these rooms of grace and fading slows that go nowhere far to high.

After breakfast we got an auto near the hotel. The driver was a senior man and he said he would be retiring soon. He told us all about the rickshaw business, how awful it was, scams and terrible loans. He brought us to an office that booked trips around Rajistan. In an air conditioned room they offered tea. We sat at a desk with a well-dressed man behind it. He told us all the things we could do, and how much they would cost. In the moment, without speaking anything of it, Achara and I decided it would be a good idea to tell people we were on our honeymoon. The people in the office congratulated us for our new bonding of the souls and gave us a cheer with a couple of beers for each. We booked a journey with a private car, over to the Taj Mahal and some other places of notable historic value. We returned to our hotel and packed our things, our new driver waited outside in his Fiat. His name was Goral. He was a severe looking man, but extremely amiable; a friendly pit-bull.

We left the city, one of the most densely populated on earth, and the land opened up to the desert. More of Aladdin. People were just someplace else, tightly packed together. We drove and I watched the land go by. Our driver Goral got talking about his family. He had recently been married. It was arranged, but he now loved her more than anything. He had a child of three months back at his home. "I may be like sandpaper, you know, sandy on the outside, only paper on the inside. Watch that I can destroy wood and even change the shape of metals." The Taj Mahal. Money. People. Walking. Watching. Money. After all, it was made by the hands of man and the purpose of its construction is debatable. For love, fame, or war, which was it? Either way it took twenty thousand people to build it. Give us twenty thousand people to build something beautifully useful, useful at least, or is art the most useful, praise to the patrons. We visited the grounds of the Taj Mahal and were given a tour by a young man that insisted he must. They made their money from people like us. He took photos of us on the famous bench, Achara and I made trite poses like the late royalties. While in a pose for a photo on a side of the main building, security enclosed. The guards declared there were to be no religious demonstrations and asked Achara to remove her shawl that had on it a golden Om. Ridiculous. Censorship. To make rules. What a bunch of bastards. I did not want to play there.

More famous forts in Rajistan. We rode around as kings in the back of that cab. Achara and I spoke. She had a good mind but was damaged from the world she was fighting. She thought I was mad to try and go against the grain but saw truth in it, for her own journey was made from the departure from the rest. "You've got to go to college one day, Prem," she said. "Then at least you'll know more of what you wish to change." After the tours of famous stuff we went to take rest at an old castle-looking place. With a view of the fort, Achara and I dined on the roof under the stars. We were the only customers to the hotel. The roof was empty. "It's strange here in India," she said, looking at a strawberry. "My life is a mess but I feel fine."" Yeah, I'm not sure I've got a life to even live besides this. I can't see home." "I haven't told my mother that I've quit my job." "She'll understand if she loves you." A silence. "I grew up a Thai girl in Germany, you know, like a stranger. My parents made me feel love, most of the time, but even with all that I grew up hating myself. Academics were the only thing to keep my mind occupied. And funny, that's what brought me here I guess. Books, books I read to prove people wrong. A way of life achieved for others." Achara was the type of girl that always looked happy, but you could tell there was something concerning her. She was self-conscious and needed some form of power for validation and there was none there. We all are guilty of that, I suppose. "What a fate that we have to feel loved," I said. "My most major fault, my love is never enough."
"How beautiful we are because of it!" she declared. We made a toast with our mugs of lemon ginger tea.

On our ride back speeding along a desert road in Rajistan I concluded that if I had never grown up alone tortured by my own indifference, I would never have become a seeker of eccentric difference, to be entertained by all life, that theater space, such a funny place, none now mattered without the experience, all up there together. Like all the other assholes. I had thought the thoughts again and made them think. I could see myself, and see all that I was capable of. It was neither the ride nor Achara that brought my state of mind to such clarity, only time. Then it was gone.

Lady takes me swimming and the currents throw me tumbling
.I beg to to warn distraction steal me as I sing so softly sitting.

We returned to Dehli mid-afternoon. I fell severely ill a little ways before entering the city and could not find the energy to move or speak properly. I lay shivering in the hotel bed. Achara paid Goral and thanked him for his services. We had become friendly. He arranged a cab free of charge to take me to the hospital. Achara sat beside me with my hand in hers, she placed a cold compress across my forehead. I felt more ill as the moments passed. I was useless and regressed into my child. Maybe I was poisoned. The hospital people brought me to a metal bed, a doctor came, I explained my condition, I was given a shot of penicillin and an I.V. of fluids. Some sort of stomach infection, they said. They released me and we returned to the hotel. We booked a train up to Haridawar. From there we'd drive back to Rishikesh. Spinning.

I forgot about my illness as we drove under the pink gates to upper Rishikesh. "Be good do good." I was back, so close to being home in the country. We booked a hotel near town. It would be best to rest before I confined myself again to the river. Beside the bustling town I stayed in bed. I slept for days and days and only got up every so often to use the bathroom or sit on the patio overlooking the Ganga. I shat blood and vomited all day and blamed myself. Paradise was outside. I wanted to die before it was taken away, so now I felt defeated. Achara would wander around town discovering things herself, a place all her own. When finally I regained my strength I was many pounds lighter but infinitely more heavy with happiness to be well again. Suffering. Relief. Bliss. Evaluation. Repeat.

I excitedly walked the streets of Rishikesh with Achara for the first time since I had been back. The river was blue and the people around familiar. A novel, another character. I had changed. As we walked along the road that led along the river, a loud yell came from behind. Bhupi ran up and nudged my back with his hand. "Hari om, Prem!" "Hari om, Bhupi!" "How long have you been back?" he asked." Only a little while." "O good, Prem, we must have lunch today. Who is your friend?" "Yes, this is Achara. I met her in Kerala. I'm going to show her Ghadughat." "O good, nice to meet you, Achara. I am Bupender." He put his hands together. "Nice to meet you, Bhupender. "The three of us walked to a nearby cafe for lunch. We ate. We spoke of Ghadughat. A strange enterprise. "Bhodi wants good work, but does not want to pay, He wants work well done but does not want to manage." "Yeah, you really can't do that. He's just an eccentric, hell figure it out." "Yes, yes, but it is my duty to take care of him." Bhupi was one of most honorable men I knew, he had helped Bhodi build his first ashram on the illegal land. Bhupi had warned him but Bhodi didn't care. It was a Utopian dream to think we can do as we wish in this world. We cannot forget the game we must play in order to succeed unless we play the role of disruptor, and who is brave enough? Bhodi didn't like any of this. Bhupi was stressed. "You know, Prem, I would not want this to happen but I may be finished helping Bhodi once he returns from Germany. His mind is lost by all the things he's thinking and not doing." He looked terrible using these words. "Well, Bhupi, I must say he is a strange man, and there are things I despise him for, but I don't know how I could ever be mad with him, so we'll see what happens." Achara sat listening to us. " It doesn't sound worth it," she said. "Why would you both be so nice to a man that is so bitter and from what I have heard narcissistic as well?" she asked. "Simply duty," Bhupi replied. And I? He seemed the most reasonable choice in this land of madness. Freedom with a touch of order from the reliable pathetic. A bit dark.

Achara and I sat in the Dev Raj cafe. We looked to the Ganga. Bhodi proudly walked by. It was different to see him a second time; he looked helpless. While away I had registered his company of hypocrisy and it made me ill. He sat down at our table."Hari om, Prem." He looked at me and then Achara with sarcastic eyes, as if to say, Oh, a woman you have with you. What a fool this child is to succumb to pleasure. A creation of my mind. "Hari om," I replied." Namaste,"

Achara said."So how have you been?" I asked, and looked to his eyes.
He was in another place. "The chai wallah up the road is trying to steal
my land and I'll be leaving to Germany soon. Do you plan on returning
to Ghadughat?" "I may return tomorrow, but I will stay in the cabanas
beside the house for some time until Achara leaves. I would like her to
come see it, would that be okay with you?" "Yes, Prem, just don't go
inviting the whole world." A reflection of myself. I become what I run
from. I take what I scorn to leave. As if humans try to grasp their
realities by creating clones from place to place. If we do not change,
something strong sleeps within us, yet if we accept change we also
accept there is a point of reference. This is from where this world has
come, sleeping dreams, our only reference.
Bhodi abruptly left for his van. Achara and I returned to our hotel. We
would journey for Ghadughat the next morning. More spinning.

Hospitals; business.

News annals; business.

People's business.

Fast man too busy to sit down for tea.

The talkers fast and finite spinning free

.Bask and be

Death be to the perpetuating clichés.

Today

your topsy-turvyl scriptless play.

Fallings

Chapter Six

Bhagat wore tight pants and walked with a flute too large for his pocket. He walked up and down the property examining plants of the gardens, meticulously removing any dirt or bug. He looked after the bamboo cabins just a ways back from where I had stayed. He and his friend Anand were disciples of the late Osho and spoke about getting fucked up on the regular. I met them briefly before passing through the fields. Achara and I took two rooms under their management, sleeping in separate huts. "It wouldn't be right for me to sleep with a woman that is not my wife in such a place," I said. I laugh. The feeling behind my decision escapes me. I don't know if I was concerned with conservative thought, respect, or just simple fear of judgment. What an idiot with all these imaginations, to be sick with complications. This picture is far too simple to draw.

Look at that lingering paint; a message on the wall.
No more than recognitions as this wet paint starts to fall.
Our business thrice removed; it is not for us to call or see.
That lingering paint no longer calls as we forgot our ancient plea.
Lost among the praise we've yearned to death to breath.
Look at this lingering paint, it is there, right there, you see.

Bhodi lay in his room. I showed Achara around the grounds. We walked by the red door I would open with love. "Come in," Bhodi whispered, noticing our presence. We entered and sat upon the old bed I had used opposite his. Achara greeted him "Namaste," she said. He ignored her and took a bite of an apple. I greeted him more loudly. "It's good to see this place, you know." I pointed around the room. "The country," I said.He looked up. "Good, Prem, good. Why don't you go and fix the garden if you wish, or just frolic around the country, whatever you like." He waved his hands.Fuck him, I thought. He's gone mad with his role. There's room for more than one on each step. We're all so stubborn. We slipped away and started for the land. The celibate monk was getting to me. He was losing the mind to religion, to the shows. My enormous mountains of reaction regarding my role excused the whole world. I'm afraid he was not losing his mind, nor I mine. Lost in the doing and making, we were not ourselves.

I have been saving money for a rainy day,

I have slaved for money this waning day,
it will rain tomorrow and I will spend it all.
I shall not lose it, use it but bend it tall.
My dainty pay.
I saved that money for this rainy day,
too bad I lost the key to the box in which I hid it.
Now the lock will not permit me no matter how hard I go and hit it.
and do you know what? A stranger found that fucking key one sunny day.
He up and drank each of my moneys away.
What now is there left for me to say?
I have saved all my fucking moneys for this here rainy day.

Achara and I tilled the garden for the afternoon. She was a lady and looked funny playing in the dirt. Still, we dug down into the earth removing rocks from the soil. We planted seeds and trees in the new section of garden and watered them well. When we finished we sat on the stone wall along the back. We ate mangoes. Bhodi hastily stepped forward. "What have you done? You put the squash to close together. Mindless. It would have been better for you to do nothing at all, you young girl," he said under his breath with anger. We left the garden be, the squash. Everything is ruined now. I've come here to have fun. Now you're going to make me leave. Why are you here? Achara poured over herself. We must all be inherently confused, she thought, or maybe she thought he was jealous that he'd gone rancid knowing that I denounced taking to the monastic life. He would tell me in the early days we met that we needed to lead our sleeping generations into fulfillment and out of miscommunication and bureaucratic masturbations. Yes, but such big ideas in the tiny minds along the petty shore. I could not dare help a man along the road. I can't subscribe to a thing and then the pit seems to deepen.

Studious underlings searching undone rhythms.
Duly trust what dogs have left while searching wonton idioms.
They say they must be busy, busy teaching theft, just as truth from
whaling Walden finally comes to set!

Bhodi went back to the house. I led Achara down by the riverside towards the confluence. "He's not a very kind man, Prem," she said, looking down at her toes sparkling in the water. "He's not, that's true. From the moment I met him he was this way, but he seems to have gotten worse. But you know I can't imagine that I know who I was when I met him. The flamboyant moody orthodox, interesting yeah, I find solace in this. The well-traveled, no matter the travel."
Why else I would ever spend time in the company of another? I want to be flabbergasted. If the earth has got a show, then fuck me I'm gonna watch from the front row. She nodded, but seemed not to think well of my words . "So what's his life about?" She asked."I never asked, really. I've overheard him speaking with others. He mentioned things in passing. He was raised by a highly conservative family, and when he met some liberals in college where he spent some time studying for architecture he dropped out to wander the United States as a sadhu-type figure with a friend. He lived in communes and did all sorts of hallucinogenics. He read Goethe, Leary, Gogol, listened to the Grateful Dead, experimented with bestiality, slept with guys, women. It's out of the question that he could be judgmental. A love of a man, though, really, when all is said. But you know I've glorified him, I glorified myself, everything. I just made him up, you know? He's always been this way. We play these roles, find one, play, don't play if you don't want to. Unless you don't know that you are already."

We came to rocks in the Riba. A good level of water fell over some stones making the water white. We removed our clothes and slowly walked to the pool. We gathered by the head of the flow and tingled in the movement. A young boy from the village walked up from nearby. He sat on a stone a ways away and closely watched us with a fat smile. He was stolen by Achara, her breasts were free, her soft light nipples hard; the boy would never see such things.

Back at the cabins, Bhagat was singing to Anand's playing of the drums. I took a shower in the stall behind my cabin. In the cold water I regretted not rooming with Achara. My nude body seemed pointless alone. Ghandi slept in a bed with young girls in order to test his devotion to his way of life. Bang, I thought. Sunset came and we took a dinner the boys cooked up. We sat in wicker chairs. A cassette tape of Bob Marley played over dusty speakers. A smoke. White stars above. Coming in from the cold. Achara and I got up to the tune and wildly danced. We threw off our shirts and twirled around. She spun and pirouetted with grace. We knew the part but knew not why. We did not know the vibrating arousal. We came together again and again and still asked for more. We knew nothing, but together it seemed fine. She took my hand and led me back to her room where we fell into one another. We pressed into our bodies. We sat up, clasped together, biting lips, and she came. Trembling soft along the lines, her flowing figure mine. I gave her all I had. I gave what I could. I lifted her and carried her up and out to the fields. We came again under the moon among the corn. We lay on our backs listening to streams of the river and whos of the owl and clattering tick tack of bugs. What now? I thought. Still, I was hungry. Damn the apple.

I feel I don't belong here, way beneath this shelled turnstile.
I think too much to think and think to think my own damn trial.
What a joke this monkey is as he writes with monkey style.
My monkey's hands would feel all the better if I could only see you smile.

I awoke early in my bed alone. I flicked a bug from off my chest. For some reason I left Achara late in the night. I would marry her, I thought, and if I did I would no longer have to participate in these games. The escapers are no better than the Brahman, I thought. The sun had just risen and the air was still cold. I threw on a dhoti and wandered through the gardens. A darkened man sat smoking beneath a mango tree out by the bathhouse. Below the heavy branches his skeleton body made love to a chillum, his long black dreads sparkled with trinkets. He wore only a fading loincloth. "This sun is new," he said, staring at me with his one good eye. "Yes, beautiful," I replied. A response that always was. It was silence we were after. The old wood block print of the monk emerging from the cave after realizing himself. Ahah. "The air is changing," I continued, and sat beside him to join the morning. He handed me the old smoke piece. We smoke classically with prayer and ritual. In lotus strange highs come and I entertained them for a long while. I returned the pipe and returned to the page.

You are the king said the kids in the yard.
You are the king as you cast your last card.
Bent past sky's last star, woven thick between the ranges of the ever-
made mar.
Wish. Wash. Wishy Whitman water wash. Walking clocked and ready
mocking; buy me a dollar.
We are the kings of the black blue empire.

"Om bolenath!" The baba yelled, and he began moving
himself into different postures. More smoking. I watched the river. Iou,
Iou. Achara came to join us. She witnessed my altered state but did not
react. She too smoked with the baba. The same way we did. The smoke
turned her from a stone to water. I left over for a patch of grass nearby
for some posture and breath.

The stone path led from the river to town strewn about
complete. Sadar's kids played with a puppy outside their house. Sajani
cooked chapati on a bed beneath the stairs leading up to the roof. Sadar
greeted Achara and me. "Hair om, G," he said, and bowed courteously,
almost falling over. He started on the bottle early. "Hari om," I said. He
was expecting us. "This is my friend Kamala," I said in Hinglish. This
was Achara's other name, born of the lotus, names, super
names. "Namaste," she said. Sadar smiled boyishly, numbly leading us
into a room beside the stairs. A familiar place. Pictures of famous
Bollywood actors were posted on the wall, Kumar Gonharva came
from a tape deck. I lit a Beedhi. Achara left the room to play with the
children, I sat with Sadar, he lit a beedhi. We stared around and said
nothing. He was always sick with silent laughter, you met his eyes and
you saw what was going on. Stoned from the drinks. Sajani came in.
She thought Achara and I were married and winked at me for being shy
and keeping it a secret. After Achara left, Sajani decided that I must
have done something very bad to have made her go. She spoke with me
no further. The world escaped her. The children tugged at Achara and

giggled; she was a rare kind to come through those parts and the order
of her Sari was wrongly dressed. How could this be, they wondered.
They fixed it up, and we took lunch. Cucumbers, rice, and onions. On
our way back through the town, in the bend, Rawat yelled my name
from a patio above the convenience store. He came down, curious of
my guest."G, your wife?" he asked, full of excitement. " No, Rawat, a
friend, Kamala. Kamala, Rawat G," "Namaste, Rawat G." She greeted
him with her hands together. "Beautiful," Rawat said through a smile.
We looked at each other for what seemed to be a while. We had
nothing to say. Rawat was taken be Achara, as was I. I was taken by
Rawat and his missing fingers and wacky wobbling stance. Achara was
taken by whatever it was she wanted. Crash. A loud noise came. Smoke
came from the community wheat-shucking machine. Rawat ran off. "A
nice man," Achara said. "I hope everything is fine." "Yes, I'm sure it
will all be fine," I said. "He's a good man and I think he knows it.
We're all less men here and more of what we should be."

A good morning by the river out there alone. Nobody outside
and the birds were walking. Weightless swathing dimming spry. I
bathed and walked up. Bhupi was out there in the distance surveying
the land, speaking with the workers. Achara was with them. I started
over for them. Bhupi caught me watching Rawat's younger daughter
working the rice fields behind the land. "Maybe you can marry her,
Prem. You seem a sensible man." He laughed and continued, "Good
dowry from Rawat." "Ridiculous, true, possibly possible, but
ridiculous. In a different life?" Man, what a life someday could take.
Rawat's daughter was a perfect bright in the yellow and worked with a
certain profound tranquility. Maybe it was she who held the answers.
Bhodi walked from the river up to where we were speaking. Salad
sprouted in the gardens. The walls to the room were up and the roof
was on track for commencement. The whole place was green. A lot of
things happening. "The meditation and yoga hall shall be over there,"
Bhodi said, pointing to an empty spot on the land across the rooms.
"And there," he said, pointing down by the riverside near the boulder.
"There shall be a deck for people to practice and lecture outdoors." For
what reason, I wondered."Yes, yes, Swami G, in time all will become
good," Bhupi said."It looks very promising," Achara complimented.
Bhodi looked at her plainly. "Prem, what do you think?" He scowled.
"It's all very nice. And the garden of sand and stone will be over here?"
"Oh yes. That will be in the center leading up to the pond. "Imagining

the place. He was set on owning the land himself. He wanted his name on the title. As it was it was primarily in the name of a society and legally under Bhupi's name. Business nonsense. Achara and I started off to the spot cleared in the forest across the river, the rumble sublime. She didn't like Bhodi. I understood, and laughed at myself for taking this role.

Sometimes there's just no place for guests when you're trying to find out what's going on. This is the way things happen, yeah, like the trees growing towards the sun out from the shade. Bhodi did not wish to see me when I was with Achara. He was bitter whenever we passed by. He looked down when we spoke. I invited him and his new friend for a discussion by a fire. He had been speaking with a depressed chef from London who was living in the compound down by the confluence. I planned a fire and some food for us to eat. I would be leaving Achara at the Haridawar station early the next day.

Birch stumps surrounded the fire. Achara and I sat across from one another. The rice fields were blacked out by the night and the moon's reflection shown clear in the river. The Englishman from the confluence arrived, his head had been recently shaved. He called himself Fenn. Fenn was concerned with the place in which he was staying, the types of people there; he said that he knew that he thought much differently than all of the them. He declared that they all acted as if they had a secret and would not tell him. He dreamed to know. He said he could not see the river. I could not see the river. To see a river once. In this time it seemed as if we wished to say, If others do not know what you're thinking, you might as well be thinking nothing at all. Bhodi walked over. London Fenn changed his way and started prodding him with all sorts of transcendental questions. Bhodi played the role of orthodox, only in these moments perhaps, far less open-minded than I had seen him other days. He began going on about how the monastic life was the real path and that celibacy was the only thing to do to in order for one to reach cosmic bliss or mental liberation. Was it this way, or had we only decided on the group of words we wished to use to settle in our limitations? Achara initiated a discussion on the nature of the universe. Each statement she made Bhodi refuted stating that she was wrong, thinking wrong. Can one think wrong? Fenn had nothing interesting to say. He kept asking, "Why?" The simple question. Simply is. But this leads no place. And even if you do know the literal answer in the form of language it does not imply one's

understanding. What simply is escapes me. Damn. On that night Bhodi
went on answering questions with complex ideas and paradigms,
backing them with facts of science and history. The settlers of teams
robbing the world. Men, no more than men, speaking righteously of
ways unknown. The lost dreamers clapping, desperately clawing for a
tangible surface. As I. As I. Another way to watch.

These judgments seem outdated with their arms gone atrophy.
Still spinning dreams mutated spun with yarns sung wavily.
After whiles upon whiles when he finally wakes to me.
He begins to lull his daring dreams with songs that sing he's ever free.

The fire died down. Bhodi and his friend wished us goodnight
and started for the river. They felt wronged, they walked away strong in
the act of mopery. Sadly, I despised Bhodi that evening, I let these
judgments color my views. A man of his nature could not take
opposition, he liked things done the way he wanted. After perfection. I
saw this fragile-minded animal for the first time that night and went
into a spin of no reference. I must have changed, I thought, but why?
He no longer fit with the upper echelon of thoughts spewing bullshit
from my left. We remained by the coals. Achara blew me a forgiving
kiss, and I smiled for her. We made our way across the grass into her
room. We crept out late and made love in the rice fields, her breasts
free and her naked hips rolling and going. The air seemed thick, and I
allowed my final moments with Achara to be stolen by thoughts. The
next morning as her train pulled up we stood in silence. She boarded,
set down her belongings, and stood by the door of the train. What was
there to say? She slowly rolled away. She waved. She disappeared. I
started for the rickshaws. Just a bit more empty. No more women to
pass my mind.

Slowly I strolled the riverside back into town above the
bridge. I went along a sandy path that led me by a long set of white
stairs going to the water. I got to a good piece of beach with some
boulders around. I sat with them in the sun, watching the kids play
cricket in the sand. Fenn was walking on a path a ways above. I called
to him. He came over and timidly sat among the stones. Fenn looked
sad, his head was down and he rubbed his thumbs in his palms. He
looked off on such a beautiful day. He was confused. It seemed to him
that this place was shallow and fake as all things anywhere embellished

with word. You could see people change their dress a day after they arrived, from polos to hemp pants and loose vests, a quick change of dress and a few words here and there added to the vocabulary. Now look. The fine efficacy of style. It made him feel the place was the game show that it was, that it all is. He told me he wanted to go back home and found the contemplative life a useless one. "Fuckin' contemplatives have no place in society." He lit a bidi.I had similar thoughts but did not wish to acknowledge them. Be cool or be a loser, be the wealth or the pauper, the positive or the negative, you play no matter, there is no dice here. I left him on the beach and left off for Ghadughat.

Commotion was all around the property when I came down into the fields. A worker fell off the roof and was rushed to the hospital. Bhodi was yelling. Workers argued with Bhupi and Bhodi. Convinced the place had evil spirits, they did not want to continue working until a ceremony was performed to remove them. It had to be done. Shit like this mattered in the country. When Bhodi finished speaking with the workers he came to the room. I was sitting in a chair by the window. He came in and began to complain about the land and all the illusion. He lost his patience and I lost my patience with him.

The passive reader seeds them sown, he comes self-satisfied.
This elastic meter to tease the bone, becomes unjustified.
Attentive behaviors chasing the throne suppose he's fails to lie.
He's bent on dangers fastened lone for these wide words to die.

We got to town. We went to collect some of Bhodi's literature from police custody. In the evening we went to the hospital about a pain in his side. A bit earlier Bhupi informed us that we needed to pick up the working man who had fallen from the roof, he had no ride and had fractured his hip. He was in a terrible state, recovering in the slums. Bhodi and I waited for a doctor to see him about his side. It was getting late, and we needed to pick up the worker and then head back before the damn closed. The road back to Ghadughat closed after sundown. It was near this time and we were still waiting for Bhodi to be seen. It was this time when he came out. He had pulled a muscle in his side, and was told to wear a brace. He refused to do so on the grounds of bad design.

We sped to the slums. Bhodi spat furiously about missing the chance to cross back. The negative escaped. He flicked on the siren outside the place to get the worker's attention. I got out from the car and slammed the door, disgusted by this illogical rudeness. I made my way through an alley and was escorted up a flight of stairs into a small room with no roof and cement floors that were lined in sawdust. The injured worker held his hip, moaning on the floor over a plate of rice given for dinner by his family. The siren rose. I ran back outside to tell him to wait some more moments. "You have no patience," I said with a dry face. He said, "We'll go anyway, Prem. We're going to miss the gate, so we'll leave him." I jumped in as not to be left in the slums for the dark. Just as the van was getting off a few men emerged from the alley running with the recovering guy in their arms. I yelled for Bhodi to stop. The worker and his wife were put in the car and we sped off. Bhodi was silent. All were silent. The gate to get over the damn was closed. They opened it back up when we arrived without asking any questions. It was the regular long while until we arrived in Ghadughat. When we parked, Bhodi got out from the car and briskly walked off. The worker was telling me something but I could not understand, my Hindi was for nothing and his accent was strong. Bhodi continued on down the hillside refusing to translate as I yelled to him. His wife and I looked at each other and laughed. The man looked lost. I carried the man in my arms down the path past the hill and through the rice fiends over the waterways back to his home, where I went up the stairs and placed him on the open roof atop a blanket. Bahador was there and he looked at me and shook his head and gave me reassurance that the world was filled with love. We smoked a bidi in silence and watched the river. When I went back to the house, Bhodi was eating in the kitchen, passing time as if nothing had happened. I said nothing and lay in bed. He was so far in his mind he didn't even realize it. He was a shallow man taken to the brim with something like the id. Sadness took me for being with him. I drifted off to sleepless dreams.

A while went and I kept more to myself without a thought. Rubbing hash. Sitting. Thought, finis. Walking. Breathing. Air. Sleeping harder. Bhodi left for Germany one afternoon. He rode off by bike. I waved goodbye with a tired face. He gave me the keys to the van and some money to look after. We spoke monotone, like breathing deeply in rain. He was a child playing the part of seeker. As was I. I waved goodbye to him as he rode down the winding hills, farewell. He

passed over the hills and I felt a weight leave me. On my way back to
the house, a neighbor called me a free man. They thought of Bhodi as a
seriously ill-tempered man that only dampened my free nature. I was to
be free, but I have always been free. Bhodi was gone and once again I
was alone in Ghadughat. With time, time to think about the monk, time
to think about the roles we played bemused. I would leave before Bhodi
returned. I did not want to see him again. I would depart.

Reign-less jumping sprawling free,
in the greatest glistening crawling seas.
Black blue lapping; swimming, me;
white blue saplings of the bhodi tree.

The morning was warm with air as sweet as honey. I lay
strewn across the steps to my room admiring the land. Anything. I
dropped a bar of sand-soap into a tin along with a washcloth and
toothbrush. I walked. I looked to my reflection in the trickling waters.
My hair had grown out and was looking a bit weathered. I bathed
where I would often watch the townswomen herd and wash their yaks.
A fine spectacle on the brink of a day. This morning I was alone. On
mornings like these, with only faint sounds of the water flowing among
the stones and birdsong, came the audible sun's rumbling rise.

I reclaimed a mango I buried in stones beneath the current
overnight to chill. I left my things and started upriver. Sitender was
sitting below a good tree a few meters above the river banks. He
motioned with his hands for me to join him. He was a good man, good
men smile when they are alone. I made my way through some blue and
yellow. Sitender sat in lotus listening to Bhimson Joshi from a tape
deck. "Hari om, friend," he said. He never learned more than a few
English terms. "Hari om, G," I said, and sat watching a deer drink from
the river. We smoked and laid back to watch. I rested my eyes and fell
into a nap. When I came to, Sitender was gone. I wandered down by a
field beside his house. He was crouching, messaging a bong tree in a
rolling motion. His hands were black with resin. He was nursing a pipe
that hung from his smile as I approached. "Ah, Namaste, my friend," he
said, his smile so large I thought his teeth might fall out. "Namascar." I
shook my head from side to side and a smile crossed the length of my
face. Here words could only slightly resemble the truth. The human
language can only go so far.

I removed the cold mango from my bag and offered half to Sitender. He accepted in silence, silence is the key, for there are no questions in silence. Sitender was removing the resin from his hands onto a piece of news paper. I started on my mango. All are guilty of being foolish at one point or another, I thought, but being consciously foolish, taking part in the act of foolery entirely aware and removed from ignorance, is that foolish to be so? Is an act merely defined by accountability or the motivations behind it. Freedom. Mango juice dripped from my chin. Sitender finished removing the resin from his hands. It is removed by rubbing your hands together creating friction. If you move too fast you will give yourself a blister. This was an excellent thing to happen for such a cause. He finished his mango. "Kala charas!" Sitender yelled, and passed me the chillum. We stoned oourselves until everything was real, everything began talking with us, even Tattoo the town dog. Tattoo was always laughing, a simple dog. I got up for a stroll and left Sitender in the brush, no goodbyes there. I sat on a rock in the river watching the sun dance across the current and fell into a daydream.

A rusted two story Gazebo rested in the center of Plaza de Sanfrasisco. It was designed by Gustave Eiffle. Cafe Tourismo was opposite the plaza along the Street de Los Lleguas. There was never too small a thing to merit an afternoon of good wine and better talk at the cafe. The women there were wealthy and had strong sex in their body language. It was middle June and Dave and I had come down from the Andes to publish an article in the local newspaper. We had a recycling project going in Los Quenes, to raise awareness among the locals. Carlos, a lawyer by trade, guitarist by spirit, came from the street and joined us for glass of Carmener. We spoke of the weekend-long ashado planned for the next week at Juan Pablo's house in Quilvo. We hadn't seen him since the last time we came down from the hills, when we went duck hunting in the dry riverbed near Romeral with the men of the Fargus family. That night we drank niache, the blood of a freshly slaughtered lamb mixed with wine and spices. The next day we went cherry picking on horseback. Carlos, Dave, and I were sipping the wine, children were playing in the plaza, school was out for lunch. Then I came back, I was in Ghadughat, in India, doing something. I started for my hammock to read Whitman for the afternoon. My visa was almost due for a renewal. Soon I would visit Nepal.

Sitender came by and he had with him two friends, each with a poorly made rucksack with a metal frame. They were on the run for a temple in the hills, a day or so away by foot. They sat on my stoop, one of them a flautist, the other a player of the tabla. They took out their instruments and improvised a song, Sitender sang. I quickly gathered some things in a pack and locked my room. Once out of town, we walked along. We kept on and passed into new scenes. A small village with chickens in the streets and old men falling into booze on porches with wicker chairs. An old bridge. Like the one downstream it had been built by the British. Its steel cables supported wooden planks that led across a deep section of the riba. We walked into lush hills. We crossed paths with country men; they smiled and looked to us with a familiar glance.

Green was everyplace, and the path was of a red soil. We had been walking the whole of the morning when I saw an elderly woman working the garden outside her low slate stone house. Sitender started up to a path leading to the home. The woman was a centurion, she was well over one hundred and well-known for it in those parts. Still, she worked her garden of ginger, the ginger she'd sown her whole life. Her braided white hair bleached from time in the country complemented her skin that was as a book of short stories. She looked at me with an almost forgiving face and then spoke with the boys for awhile. Sitender informed me that she wanted me to know that my eyes looked as the sky does when the sun is rising in winter. She led us over to a fresh spring where the water was sweet. She slowly nodded to the side as we thanked her, as if she would never see us again. At the top of a hill we could see down near Ghadughat and down past the confluence to Rishikesh. We sat beside one another on the steps leading to the temple. One of Sitender's friends sliced a papaya and divided it up among us. The Pujari came out from the temple, an old friend of Sitender's. He laughed and gave us all some sweets. Clouds swept in and from under the entranceway we watched the land come with rain. The clouds quickly left and the sun went to dry and the earth breathed. All the birds were out and the trees stretched out to take rest after their drink. The soil was moist and the bugs moved about. I took some bitter nut for chewing.

Euphoric blasphemies, the button come undone.

Sued on sued fantasies, as John Smith kills the fun.
They paid us for these fallacies so by the riff they run.
We're rich now and smoking, in the chamber of this gun.

Around our rest spot before sunset, a group of children approached us. The eldest spoke English well. "Why are you not married, sir?" he asked, smiling and looking back to his friends. "What is love, sir?" one of his friends asked with him translating. "Tell us about New York city and freedom," another said through the eldest. I did not not how to answer them. Bashfully I told them that they were all good things but what they had here is what caught me the most. They ran off and gathered us wood for a fire. We made a nice fire. We played a game of hoops with the children, almost like horseshoes but there was no space in the ring being thrown. The children left for their homes. We smoked and laughed and laid down for bed. Our heads rested outside a plastic covering, and the stars took me to sleep far away someplace. We returned too soon. The whole place got small. Go north, I thought, then I will be happy.

On the grass that lined the river Sitender worked binding bamboo. I walked to him. "Let's go north upon my return from Nepal. I'll get you on the money," I said. He didn't have the money to do such things. He was delighted and cackling with laughter. He pushed me into a nearby pool of water, then jumped in himself. I left for town really restless after that. So I rented a motorcycle. Bhupi's friend arranged an Enfield. I met him for it in the center of lower town. I had never ridden a motorcycle, but I told him I had, of course. The man looked at me suspiciously as I slowly mounted the bike. When I asked him how to start it, his face turned red. I told him I had merely been accustomed to different bikes back west. He seemed satisfied with this and showed me how to take it from neutral to first. I sped off into the crowded streets. The moment I turned a corner I stalled the bike in the middle of traffic. I couldn't start it. I was shifting slow with the throttle again and again. Laughter. A rickshaw driver jumped from his car and tapped his hand on the handle bars and smiled. "First time riding a bike, huh?"
"It is," I laughed. He explained in a dance how to go and helped me off. He clapped his hands. I got out of town. No more people. Cars. Noise. Good dirt followed along the cliff up the water. I rode back toward the fields, past the Swiss man's house and past Sitender's land. I rode farther down over the bridge and on towards the north. I passed the

villages and the country kept up after that, the Riba went wide to a dry bed of large stones, and the small stream snaked its way through.

       I felt content moving along. I had seen so many others riding along happy looking. I was plagued with thought. It had been the reason to go riding in the hills. My findings of morose nature grew dark thoughts. I rode disappointed in the fact that I never rose to a role back home. School had never mattered, I never took a role. I would have liked to blame it on life for acquainting me with such characters. We may pursue the one across the room for advice but only with our own hands may we place the bet. Something yelled and I felt obliged to use emotion, along with all the other things, I didn't care at all, not at all, only those millions of characters. Like a child again, slowly I misplaced some of my arrogance. Ironically, becoming more satisfied was merely losing satisfaction altogether. The romantic perceptions of a young man from an affluent neighborhood, from the dew and all other things.

       I left town by train over by the Indian Nepalese border. For the ride I had with me one of Robert Bly's pieces, a little book on the human shadow. I'd had it with me since my arrival in India. I got it when I met him; it was a signed copy. I visited Minnesota while I was a freshman in high school to attend what Bly called the Men's Conference. Men read poetry, they sang and spoke about being men. At the end of the conference we were lead through an African tribal ceremony by a tribal leader. It was a ceremony to cross boys into manhood. In this instance, it was the symbolism they were after. The men there spoke vigorously of catharsis. I was the youngest of about fifty. We each dug ourselves a grave-size ditch deep enough to lay in, submerged by earth with only our heads remaining above ground. The graves were dug in a circle, a smaller circle was made within where a fire would be lit. The tribal leader led us from a nearby lake in a parade of drumming and chanting. We removed our clothes and each person buried the next into their graves. The soil was cold from midwinter air. Each of us still and silent gazing for a long while buried in the earth. The fire was lit. We lay in this symbolic womb of the mother earth. A regression into the women from which we had all come. We were removed from the soil and marched back to the lake where we were submerged beneath the water, a cleansing. Naked, we danced around the fire, chanting and drumming until the late night came and the moon was no longer.

I sat on the train thinking about the essence of all of this jargon. The train stopped, we were in the middle of flooded rice fields. A young boy had fallen through the walkway that leads you from one car to the next. He had been crushed by the weight of the metal wheels on the tracks. Great crowds of people were on all sides of the train. I was alone in my bunk. People were screaming, but they had no one to blame. I wept in my hands like a boy. I don't think it was the other boy I was crying for. I cried for me. I was lonely, and when the quick hand of death showed its presence I became aware of my profound aloneness. My own mind was far beyond my heart. It was she, and her whisper soothed my calloused ears.

An open Mahindra took me from the station to the border. I got my passport stamped at the dirty place and walked across into Nepal. A small border town. Booze. Spice. Yelling. A man tried to sell me a woman. Fire. I would travel for Pokhara, a city nestled in view of the Annapurna mountain range. I boarded an old overbooked bus and sat between six others. Fresh in the A.M. the town of Pokhara was empty. I walked from the bus station into the town and found a nice guesthouse in walking distance to the lake with a view of the mountains. I fell asleep on my bed with the sun from the window shining on my back. I awoke and wandered over to a nearby cafe, a family run place. I ordered some eggs and fresh bread. A flamboyant in a long beard sat across from me. The tables were communal. I grabbed a paper and read the news. I hadn't done such things in many months. Odd strange dramas around the world. The news was money and it didn't matter, unless of course it did. The economic crash of the United States, Obama in his first one hundred days. I put down the paper and laughed, and the man across from me asked what was funny. I told him it seemed that the news had gone and made it out to be like the world was on fire. Yet there we were in the Nepal enjoying eggs in view of the Himalayas. I wondered how many people find what they are looking for. I started my way down to the lake for a swim.

I swam across the lake and admired the town. All the things there had truth. The cliché ran deep enough, fuck it. The Nepalese were beautiful, the woman strong and confident with striking features, the men short and built for speed. Children swam by the beach, the young kids ditching school all gathered by the lakeside under some shade. I swam back to finish reading Bly's book on the human shadow. My funds were gone. I had gone a heavy time with little thought and the whole idea of money had escaped. I did nothing for the luck that took me, but I couldn't very well go anywhere with no money or stay anywhere for that matter. With my last Nepalese rupees I ventured out and purchased bidis, beer, a red clothbound book of pages, and some pencils. I made a phone call to my father asking him if he could wire me some money. He kindly said money could be sent, but no sooner than three days. With that call I left back for my room.

Around evening time I wandered down to that family cafe with some change from the bottom of my bag and got a plate of rice with soup. I wrote and laughed and whetted the eyes from it. Me and my imagined self, having no effect on anyone or anything, changing no rules nor adding new ones, for why was this man here then, I asked. No money, the funding of breath. Youth is simplicity, we are and always will be every man from all ages, thoughts of man, from what is and has been before. A wasteful analysis parted by the lobes. A flowery few steps we frolic all together. An elderly that I'd seen around the cafe moved across from me. He was of the mountain and had that look people get when they don't care for nothin', and he looked around like some sort of cat and then into my eyes. We can only be as good as the next man. We can only be good ourselves. The smile that starts revolution. To be without collision. To be stolen be reaction. He offered a place on his land. He had a farmhouse not too far, I would sleep in the guest shed beside the fields of corn. I followed him through the hills to his home.

A hand of nights. I awoke early and looked over the fields and then onto the mountains. We drank whisky. His kids had died a while back. He was a sad and quiet man and I ran away from the earth on his land of kindness. A light book written in a dark state of mind. Back in the kingdoms of reality, reaction means nothing, cliché. A novelty to laughing drunks, perhaps. A slap on the shoulder for being bold. Everybody.

Manu hunting,
Hey you Manu,
Denounce with sweet derision; all the funning dogs smeared with

Indecision, the desire for money, idols, mere religions,with the hawks
Height but eyes of pigeonsI've robbed you, yes, robbed you Manu.
Prepare your succulent tides.I shall not ever lick the air that leads your
ponderous lies.

It all goes as it goes when it is, yeah, and yeah John we do all want to change the world. I waited for a train to Delhi. It was running late a few hours. On the platform an Australian played Marcy Playground on a Ucayali, "One More Suicide." The station master passed, I'd spoken with him before. He pointed to a train pulling up on track two. I ran across the first track to the second and boarded my assigned car. It was night by the time the ticket master came by. I showed him my ticket and he gave me a confused look; he glanced at me and then again at the ticket. I had boarded the wrong train, the train I was riding was headed east, the opposite direction of Delhi. The train I was on was leading towards Varanasi. He handed back my ticket. I would sleep on the floor, the train was due to be full next stop, but a guy across overheard my dilemma. A student of engineering. He shared his bench with me when the night came. From my bag I removed a ball of charras the size of a good marble and chewed it up and scribbled youth.

He's blindly passing among the others as the driftwood on the oceans,
as a lover kindly splashing those ones who dare ever try and provoke
him.
Waves wild with wanion wrox out in the sun.
He had to join them 'till all the dancers dance's danced and came
undone

I arrived before the sun and again found my way through the cobblestone alleyways to a hostel on the banks. I got a room and awoke in the cold water. I sat on the floor. It was not necessary to do anything. There was no rush. But I felt rushed there and did not see. Animals should be content in doing nothing, look at cats, I thought. Do as others do, one man in the crowd runs faster then the rest. I started up to the roof to the sunrise.

Two lightly plucked fines lay back admiring the rising sun. I sat a ways from them on the edge of the roof. My feet dangled over the streets below. Dangling man, I thought, but not even a war. The city came alive. People bathing, praying to the river and the sun on the rise. Clothes washed on the rocks. Boats were out. Flowers floated down the river. Smoke from the burning ghats rose. A sweet voice came to my ear. "Come and sit with us," one of them said. I strolled over. We cuddled close and watched the sunrise. Not a word was spoken; only on departing did I thank them for the company. I started for the river to cross. The both of them stayed up there, the both of them beautiful.

Across the Ganga I swam, to the sandy beds parallel to the city. I walked along and walked along and mused for my own day. Going this way and that, the better. Breaking apart and losing the minds. Separation in ways we'll never see. Going this way and simple, suffer if you forget yourself. Separation in ways we'll never know. Present sound and weep with only, the limbo-less. Here we come again, may we end this of what we all know to end. I went back and up on some stairs over to the burning ghats. The epicureans, the renunciates, the regulars, and the others. Local girls shyly passed me by. They burned. Orderlies set up the pyres. Ghee placed. A place that hadn't changed since the second millennia before. Treating life like the familiar friend that she is.

Woody Allen, this sardonic existentialist. Try reading Allen's material after you read some literature on Vedantic philosophy and trans-personal psychology, see where that gets your state of mind. And yes, the banal nature of this absurd idea, Allen himself might say such a thing in a movement of comedy. Was it comedy I was after there? It was all quite comedic. Life is funny. Cliché is funny but still the truest of ways. I wonder if Woody still sees truth in his words. In mine I hear only drops of dim truth. Bob Dylan once said he doesn't know the man who wrote "Like a Rolling Stone." I finished reading side-effects and made my way out for lunch.

Those figures who had generously invited me to warmth were sitting outside of a small dhaba sipping tea upon wooden stools. I invited myself to sit beside them again. The epitome of beauty. Real beauty, free from sunder, this natural state. Both looked practiced with posture, their bodies the way they wanted to be. One had short blond hair with a long wave of curl, green eyes with a speck of orange in each of them. Freckles danced about her nose. The other had long brown hair that flowed to her perky breasts below the cotton. Strong cheek bones. Sandy eyes. They were dressed of the place and seemed to say that all of their questions had been answered and now they merely wished to sit around and be. You fine flowing breeze of a good walker. Inspiration.

I smoke a beedi and looked over the rooftops. I was wasted to the future. I was satisfied watching this place. The upper lip told me she was nervous but still wished to continue. The sun was just about gone. I used an old wooden fruit box as a chair. Those two girls came up the stairs and sat beside me. What the fuck is our generation I thought. "How may we be defined, as a generation?" I asked without wit. She looked at me funny for this silly question. "I would say we may be undefinable," said the one with the freckled nose. "But there is a word for everything. We are everything that has ever been before," said the other. "Yeah, the collective impact of ideas, but we have to maintain that now we can know something with the touch of a key but still people sit in ignorance. We can have a future like the movies but nobody's got the cash. There are social demographic conglomerates that can get us all onto one page of facts but we do not know ourselves and cannot rightly connect with others. So we're the children with keys, that's a good song. Kids with guns." We hummed it. "The Karma sum." Laughter. "We can do whatever the fuck we wish, but do we wish anymore? Materialism has got us. Can we not hold five million dollars and remember why it was that we came to this point," she said, smiling. " I guess it doesn't matter really." "As much as anything else it doesn't," said the dark haired girl. I'm chasing the Ferrari with clichés here. "It's tea and lemon," she said. I laughed and agreed. I looked from and not from all at the minutia of the moments. The cups of tea I'[d told to fuck off and forgot haunted my mind with their aroma and style with the unspeakable. To smell the wind and feel breeze without a care. They spoke about the city on the roof and enjoyed us with words that had no grounds. Yellow leaves.

I woke with the sun and walked to the bathing ghats where I found a rower. He brought me upriver to float back down. I helped him a short while; his eyes were glazed and he looked tired. Their life's work there. Generation to generation, generation. The life of a boatman. Rowing people up and down in old wooden boats. A swimmer drowned in the front of us, he was floating on his stomach as we passed. The whole crowd swam away; the corpse is reserved for the lowest class. We kept on up the river. By the riverside. Breath. Without lines. Stop thinking. You. From where did your wink come from? Now I know. Cease all reactions of the mind and simply be in nothing. Urge strikes. It was about time to head back. Whimsical and arbitrary natures took me away. I left for Rishikesh.

A floundering spice I smelled across the air told me of the compelling confusions beneath the hurling tribes, torn beaten and crushed back into all them peoples sitting on my mind.
About the bleeding contusions from that red curling knife.
From when it stuck one of those lovelies and now he cries every night.
About the wielding delusions at the helm of these tides;
 to call them all out from eternity and forget age and demise.
 My dear friend there is no place where the young men dawn to die.

What Side of the River

Chapter Seven

A message in funny package.
Hankering to disperse this last Lincoln visage.

The land withered brown. Construction ceased. Wild growth
sprung up all around, more cannabis. Nature reclaimed her land fast.
Bahador slept on a cherpoi under a mango tree. He squinted his eyes at
me and threw up his hands and shrugged his shoulders. He smiled and
smoked, he smoked as he smiled. Back at him I smiled. Sadar came by.
Bhupi had come down with jaundice after I left. Bhupi was a lovely
man. But something gave me the feeling I should get going, get going
the fuck out of there, someplace, it was all the same. I knew it, too.
Around once more to catch the ring.

Love sky, blue sky, up sky here.
Mumbling my mambo; up sky dear.

Pilgrims lined the streets. Town had been filled with them,
pilgrims from all over, trekking from the temple of Siva up on
Neelkanth road, past Uterkasi on to Gumouk, the head of the Ganga.
Decorous tents served food to the travelers. Orange decorated the road
north. I got a tea and watched the road. These people, all types of
people, demanding faces upon their bout of freedom, away from the
dance of wealth that doesn't give a fuck about them. I sipped my tea. A
kid threw up from walking too much. Some well-dressed people from
Dheli walked by. They had managed to get away from the grind, but

had rushed by it all. Where were they going? Gentlemen carried elderly women on their backs. I returned to my room to watch birds from the stoop.

Nearby I walked across the leaf-strewn soil. Below the trees I was grand. I must travel North, I said. I have missed something. I wandered back to the room. I dazedly looked at the envelope of money Bhodi left me to watch over. It is all the same, I thought. This money? Who's money? This, that, and the other. I took the money, placed it in my pocket, and returned to the river. Later I would give that money to a family man I saw, he had a few good looking kids and a kindly faced wife. They were dressed as well as their wallets would allow, which was little, but such gentleness, they brought light around the train. The father wore an old grey blazer with holes from wear. It was on a train going someplace where I left him with the cash. I put it in his lap and ran off for my stop. I was satisfied. I was not the money, nor was Bhodi, he took it from the whites who wanted freedom while still enslaved. It was all very pointless to me.

I started for the land of Sitender. The money skipped my mind. The bastard suits shall remain cold. Just a ways up the river Sitender and his friends gathered, crazy with dance and laughter. They were building a simple sunroom atop a cement platform. A half completed canopy made from bamboo and rope covered an area large enough for a good few to enjoy. I offered my hand in service and finished with them shortly after. We sat under shade sipping cold ground water. Noise of the tape deck played. It went dead. Music, it seemed always to be playing. One of them leapt up and began going through some things in the house. He reemerged with a long electric wire with two coat hangers strapped to one side. He walked across the property and threw the two cables over the overhead wires. On the first shot he got one on the neutral and the other on the hot. A skilled throw. The music returned. We went on dancing barefoot in long green grass. With grinning eyes, "North," I said. Sitender merrily swayed at the idea I implied with this simple word. We would go north. It seemed the most reasonable thing to do. We would take the ambulance, take turns driving and sleep in the back.

The next day the old ambulance got on its way along the carved hills running to the Ganga. On our way out, the villagers shouted after us to have a swell, safe, and happy journey. Electric with the jitters, north, I assumed that the both of us were after the end. On the way out an ancient potbellied man filled the tires with air, checked the brakes, and helped us to fasten a side panel that had been falling off. Incense burned. We kept on. The tape deck played. We drove along the cliffs. There are things we do when we need them done, we have things done when what we do is finished. Sitender leaned over smiling and revealed a good brick of hash. He had rubbed the bong trees all season and had a great personal collection of the resin. I laughed and said in Hindi, "Out of mind, out of body." We spoke nothing tangible and rode along passing a hollowed beedi.

Through the empty hills we bounced around with clean sounds of tabla booming from the raspy black box. Clouds and the blue sky lined the ridged mountains, soft greens colored the earth below. I could hear her. I was awed. A loud life. Two empty-minded sadhus flagged us down. We swept them up and kept on. More music played. Ethereal conversations mentioning only bits of the day through the wincing eyes and carless attires. Before they left off they fed us some ladu with clove. We passed through Uterkasi. The old place I visited with my father seemed dead. It was no longer enough. I passed it by without a thought of difference. We would go as far north as the light would allow.

Before the setting sun we rolled into a dhaba lot for some rest. A man with one arm came to greet us. He set down a few blankets in view of the river. I walked down the hill and bath. It was colder here and clear. I drank. I returned and the one-armed man was swinging around his stump, singing. He lost it in a climbing accident. He said he lost himself when he lost the arm so he moved into the hills. He became sad, then even more so when he discovered that it was his arm that was deciding whether or not he was happy and it no longer existed. He moved here for solace and after five years found happiness. We left him. He was free. We kept on further. The further we went, the lighter we felt. After the sun we came to an opening in a valley. A small village was there. We parked beside a hotel hanging over hills falling to the river. Smoke from surrounding houses filled the air with the clean smell of fresh wood on fire. Both without proper words, we got out in the open air and started for the hotel for food and conversation.

Three ageless guys sat on a blue bench beside a crumbling table. They shared bags of wine between themselves. Each was wrapped in a blanket kissing a beedi. Their expressions called for bliss, laughing shivers, and other good things. We sat across the way as they discussed the United States. My face was covered with cloth for warmth, my white skin hidden. They spoke about the busy men, the busy men making busy things to busy us all, the West blindly following wealth and India blindly following the West. "An eternity of flipping," one said with a professorial tone. "Not a handful of men are awake enough. If there were, they'd be here already," another said. "Silly white superstar teens all after Obama. His slogan caught the young and restless," another said with an angry jeer. I watched. Indeed these novelty presidents catch youth away from the reality of revolution. Change under oath, under the leaders, over the power. "Look at all these fools joining the party fucking each other when their bitch is elected." He'd gone drunk and sad truths escaped. We were traveling to the end where the egos went to die. I got a bag of wine myself. I was drunk. In the altitude we spoke. We grew tired of the voices and returned to the van. Bundled up and spinning, Sitender vomited out the window. He drank too much for this place. Sick with laughter, I wrote.

No matter how much he takes the eyes shan't ever shade.
Be it later, now or then, He'll entertain this grand parade,
repair the broken lights in this stumbling drunks arcade,
and finally when you know it all too well, you shall fall upon the sharp
blade that writes this place to tell.

I fall asleep looking the condensation collecting on the windows. I awoke the next morning with the sun. Rolled up tight beneath my blankets, I slid open the window and took a moment with air clear as glass over spring blades of grass.

The three men we consumed the evening prior sat outside the hotel huddled together. I waved to them as we drove off further into Himalayeh, and they bowed their heads. The sun was far from its zenith when we arrived at a village by the name of H. It was a well known place for its hand-rolled braids of hash. We sat down at an open cafe on the street for tea. The ground was old chipping cement that had been painted red. The chairs and tables were of a dark wood striped green years before. Across the room sat an elderly tightly sipping his tea. We asked around for some hash. The owner of the place laughed and pointed to his belly. The owner of the cafe. He invited both of us to follow him to his store across the road. The man showed us to a table, and then he placed a rolled up blanket with plastic lining before us and spread it out. Hash braids lay about. He helped us to pick out some that looked exceptionally nice. As many as we could fit in our hands. Back at the cafe we took a chillum with chi and parathas. A few men read the paper and incrementally said witty remarks to Sitender or I as they read. All sipped and smoked in the mood of morning. We kept on towards the north.

Soon the road grew rough and the going got slower. The concentration of Pilgrims increased. Music played. We had been riding for a bit of the morning when we came upon a gorge crossing. Sitender parked the van between some trees and went to observe the land. High walls of rock fell into a raging river far below. Old moss grew on the lonely stones, conifers all around us. Sitender and I silently smelled the place as we lay across a small crack waist wide that went far down to the water. The earth moves and the rumbles of revolution were obvious. We peeled ourselves from the vein.

Two eyes met mine as we rolled into town. A sadhu nearby sat upright in the dark. I removed myself from the van and walked to the entrance of his shanty house. The man motioned for me to enter; I sat beside him atop a wool blanket. Our breaths trailed before us. I laughed the silent dog's laugh. We smoked as he fried up some simple grains. Sistender joined us. The two spoke in a deep Garwali, a mountain tongue I had no understanding of. We sipped chi, chilled wind from the outside made a whistle as it passed by. I left the two to gather proper documentation to travel on into the mountains by foot. I stood with a group of Indian men waiting for the forest department to open. All of them shook their heads side to side upon my arrival. Jovially they crowded around me and enquired of my place of birth. "Good of you to come, this is home you know," one said. The group was merely a bunch of Indians who happened to be in the same place, somewhere other pilgrims on the trek. Some were in orange, some in white, others in street clothes. A young man from the group pulled out a chillum and began passing it around. We smoked and held good conversation about Mother Nature. I told them how to say Mother Nature in Spanish and they all repeated it amongst themselves, slapping their knees in laughter. When the department opened, a dark bearded man called me into the office. I sat down on a metal chair as he handed me some documents to sign. I signed for Sitender and myself and was given two permits lasting a week. I gave my farewells to the men who had given me good company and returned to the ambulance. Sitender was sitting inside on the floor peeling red carrots listening to Bimson Joshi.

You deepen in the argyle fight and go kill off the milkman.
You weep at closing still but rile despite my kill of ilk men.
This absurd lightless life of timid manner, wasted touch from fear.
You keep life light within your hand and let none the other near.

We would start off for the trail early the next day. It was a day's hike to the first station. I left Sitender and went to look around the town. A waterfall went over sand-colored boulders in the middle of town. I crossed a bridge nearby and stood feeling the rumbles of the ground beneath. I saw a great hill in the distance and wished to climb it. Before the hill were small residential houses, all had cooking fires burning within. I found a local looking man and asked him where I might find an entrance to climb. He led me behind his house and showed me to a small trail. I climbed a ways up and sat atop a boulder that rested on a steep slope. A good view of the town was before me. The waterfalls, ashrams, a famous temple many go to see. It was silent, like dusk in winter, the air seemed sharp, images seemed more clear there, crisp everything. Ripe greens and blues, peeling barks from the surrounding trees. Low lying bushes still a bit damp from the morning dew. I sat and thought, like when people recount experiences of near death, my life flashed before me in quick successions of feeling up my spine into my heart. I didn't know what to think of that I thought. Where had I come for all of this? I looked for home so far away. Dreams went slow during sleep, years I may never have again crossed my mind, yet I thought even in my sleep, just as well; may the imagination be nothing less than reality.

Ghandi sir, peace sayers sir, ideas for the soul, when will we feel your
worth and share this here kingdoms knoll.

Marley sir, dream singers sir, tones remind us well, when will we stop this drooling and paint our heaven done pastel.

Rumi sir, word slingers sir, definitions gone to bed, when will we end these perceptions floating round our little heads.

By dawn we passed by the trail checkpoint a ways up from the forest department. A few made their way, through the pines and gray stone. I walked a few lengths ahead of Sitender. A day of hiking and we would reach the next station. As I walked, my mind issued me an episode of contempt. It was those bastards who tried to ruin Dostoyevsky, I thought, those months they locked him in that silent room. It seems they did him well, like a thief stealing one's debts. Is there only revolution after such things, one step forward two steps back? Could utopia never be realized because of our sick disarray? I thought more, of the people who come with stories, big spacious stories, these common people who merely present problems without a thought of solutions, the bickering tabloid. What the fuck was I thinking? How terrible the sun for shining upon me. I felt ill from being so cerebral, so vulgar and cerebral. I let Sitender catch up to my side, we broke from the path to a group of flat rocks to rest our feet. No more thoughts. The river was below us and we listened and watched its water going away and going away. We agreed to not stop walking until we reached the sleeping station. We kept on up the trail in a silent manner.

With day nearly spent, we came upon a trail leading down into a valley speckled with huts. We started for a group of low-lying stone buildings. The blue sky was shielded by light rain clouds and the air was moist. Sitender and I walked to an open shed closest the river to see about a room. A man with caretaker qualities who helped run the rest house welcomed us to the mountains. He gave me a red carrot and pointed to a layout of communal rooms. Within were small rooms with smaller wooden doors. Inside, the bed covered the whole floor. The ceiling was too low to stand. It was perfect and seemed like a fancy cave. I was warm in there, swimming in the womb. Sitender and I were in ecstasy. An almond or two. A Japanese entered the room. He'd arrived only moments before us. He looked well. The three of us passed around a chillum. We conversed over topics of the life. How I loved this place. How they loved this place without a care. The innocuous careless. Everything seemed light. If you weren't careful, it seemed time passed by like it never happened and might never happen again.

We slept without sleeping a wink.

-A reaction: bang; everything escapes.

"Give me your Ferrari," said the old man.
The young desert suit winced to the sky. "Then will I be happy?" he asked.
"Yes," spoke the old man. "Then you will be free."

It was only the room and nobody cared, a few men wide and a big man long. I looked around, the only one awake. Sitender was at my side, his hair curled up from beneath his hat. Three others slept. A quiet one snored "Coo." Wind came on through the window. I uncovered myself and sat up, warming my hands with a slow breath. Chipping red paint on the walls had begun to sweat in the evening; I peeled off a piece and folded it over itself. I gained strength and stepped over the bodies mid-slumber for the acquisition of boots and a hard wool coat. In the dark hallway, I listened as people stirred in their rooms. Light from a cooking fire slipped through the cracks of a wooden door. It followed me outside into the shadows of Shiv Ling Peak. The sun had not yet beaten the mountain's height. I stood by a wall with a knee up and an elbow down to rest in the open cold. Just five years before I was sitting in a room made up of plastic arrangements. A special education school designed for kids that lacked the proper wherewithal to function in the average public setting. I was then surrounded by my lack of decisions and was lost to my own self imagined. Now I sat surrounded by my own free will.

A man wrapped in blankets emerged from the low building. He came to my side and our mouths left trails of vapor in the air. He greeted me. "Namascar," he roughly said. He was old and it seemed to me that the long gray beard he sported said nothing more than he was a kind man that knew of things that I did not."Namascar," I lightly replied.He calmly produced an orange from a satchel that hung low at his side. He then removed a chillum, the clay cylinder used for the pretty purpose of smoking, and an abalone shell case. From this he took a portion of hash and tobacco and carefully rolled them together. After wrapping the base with cloth he ignited the matter and offered it to me in silence. I smoked but it wasn't the escape we were after, we already were as far away as we could ever be. The river below moved rocks in the current, a slight tumbling clatter. The air grew dark with warmth as we dived farther. We passed it round and the ember died. We ate that orange a half each all at once, just like the monkeys would. "Om namah siviah," he said, putting his hands together with a slight bow."Om G," I replied, and gave a greatly wicked closed smile. He walked off, and if it could be so, a mountain goat looked toward my direction in the distance. My mind flowed south as I started over for it by the river down a ways. I splashed a bit of water on my face and took to looking at where my life had brought me. "Nothing here but us," I whispered with a smile, but it was with a bit of sadness that I spoke.

I returned back to the wall and that young Japanese man with poorly hemmed pants that Sitender and I met the day before was sitting there. Shortly before, he had wandered the lawless district of the Hindu Kush. His name was Minori. We did not speak then; he enjoyed the silence just as much as I. Sitender came out gave me a pat on the shoulder. The three of us sat together in breath with no reason for the idea of thoughts to enter, we were everyone and everything as we watched behind us for the human dogs that would never come back. Just four years before I sat useless, crying into my hands wondering why I was not as the others, why hatred was so, how one way could be more correct than another. My own estrangement from the true exposition of feelings broke my heart. Inner dramatics expounded to outward negativity, my sadness and constant remorse, my unscrupulous urges to feel loved, self-imposed violence and rage. Years in special education and years removed from education altogether.

The breakfast bell sounded and slowly we made our way to the dining hall. A room open to the elements, where lines of people sat cross-legged before empty tali plates. A priest came around and gave each person a metal cup with morning Chai. Another grizzly-looking man in an oversized suit jacket announced that there was to be no breakfast this day, another night would have to come for stock to arrive. None of us minded; back at the room we sat curled up in blankets, smiling with a hungry laughter. Thoughts of man came, for no reason wishing to fly and then the Wright brothers came. These dreamed-up dreamers demanding imaginations to speak truth. Still, after a round of hash and talk of times, wasted times and time again. Sitender felt ill from the altitude; he would have to stay behind. Minori and I would journey the glacier alone.

We set off to what we thought we knew to do. We walked up
to where we thought we could see a truth, to see some last fires before
we ourselves were lost to the smoke. It was all saturated with fine
colors on the way out for Gaumukh, the cow face, the headwaters of the
Ganga, sharp tones of pristine originality. Along it all but us sadhus sat
in caves with their eyes shining in the darkness, and a good glow came
from the embers of their fires. We had gone up for a bit, we'd gone
high, the breath went thick and the air went thin but still we walked
easy and whistled like birds without tunes. A fair piece of day it took.
We made it up to where the Ganga flowed from beneath a wall of ice.
Gaumukh, from where the river comes. The vein that nurtures
something like a billion bodies. A temple fashioned from stone lay
beside it. Within it a man in an orange robe sat meditating towards the
north, his flat face content and hardened from the cold. Prayer flags
flapped in the wind. I had a seat on a low rock and went over my state.
I did not wish to leave. I felt of home and saw it most in these scenes.
All the love I'd ever learned to see and all the words I learned to speak
had nothing but a laugh to say. The land and I were intimate and with
her I confessed to the perils of totality. I in an angry passion still
stumbling with simple self-interpretations knew not where my
contentment had arisen and excused it only with the land.

Minori was sitting just a ways away. I am close now, and can
leave from here, I thought. There were no games and I wished only to
continue, my legs were fine. I called over for Minori to continue
beyond the cow face farther above the riverhead. We were alone as the
path disappeared behind us along with all the other things. The terrain
rose and fell with the melted ice. Loose stone lay scattered across the
valley. Towering buttresses of stone enclosed us, shining pink in the
sun. The path drifted off left and came upon a dry riverbed of fine
white sand. It must have come from above. We were so small to speak.
We were finished. "What do you think?" Minori whispered. "Nothing,
nothing at all." We laughed into our hands and kept on up along until
the sun was above us in the sky. We came upon a break in the glacier
where a torrent flowed down a mountainside boring below it. Beside
these monsters rose a cliff that defied our scale. A tongue of its water
went with flailing wings into my pit of woe.

Minori took a bit of Hash out and placed it in the center of my outreached palm. I crumbed it with match, Minori rolled up with a local paper. We passed it round but before it could finish I left off alone into the sky. I walked alone and deeply confided in myself the curiosity of how I had come to such a place. Just two years before I was failing out of high school and blacking out on the weekends without a single thought of difference. Now here I was in the Himalayas of India contemplating a spiritually implied suicide. This walk aloft drove an inspiration into me. It was to see with my own eye the river smashing down beneath my feet. Mindless decisions of the uppermost importance. Minori stayed behind as I ascended the nearly vertical wall flanking the cliff. When I nodded him my purposed direction he shrugged with a vicious grin. I am only what I make to do, so what am I when I make nothing? Steadily I followed the steep dune of eroded rock and clung to it, making my way farther along its ridge. Fear slowly dissipated the further on I went, until I could go no further. I stopped, home, just where it all stops across the way. Silence, all else left the mind like the loudest crack floating down to earth even after the last brown leaves have fallen. Actions free from consequence. I seemed finished. Finis. So I was calm though I knew I grasped this earth so frail, this body of mundane. And as I lay and watched the soiled water floundering towards a darkness too many lengths below, I felt a faint spray wild and free from the river. Upright, I closed my eyes. Be to it my friend as the friend and find freedom. With the winds my face was gone and my hands still, my gaze opened and by the time my vision had come it was no longer. I stared, there! I was blind to being's end, truth, the unimaginable contemplation of the finis mind. The vixen so tantalizing, the warm blanket on a cold winter's night. The last cherry on the tree in an orchard of apples.

In an option squandered by imaginations I went effortlessly falling, emerging out the other side a god. It was the thoughts of this life and the veritable insignificance of its ways that polluted my idea. Then a death we know nothing of, a death that brings us life, a death that takes us from a place that we may never return. A death we love for and a death we kill for. It is so simple yet infinitely complex to ponder these universal things; I am as you are if you are who you be. To rest in the stars and gaze upon the rest with weary eyes, back to sleep for one more dream. But do not sleep too hard or fall into the fantastic, for I hear the ego murdered man's true inhibitions. We reply with only silence and sickly seek the place from where our friend Eden came without a thought of difference. To waste a life, the contemporary form of death. A wink of air in this windless room; he is stuck beyond the mind. The anticipatory lovers, far past and removed from the omitted empathy unpersonalized and crying within jealousy of the true feelings. The ambitious monks with the played out psycho-dramatics and the all too serious melancholic comedians. Now the void calls and we have the courage to respond, if it be courage one needs to do such things, to be man, immortal man.

Asked he honestly:
Are we atop the serpent's crown, or just mere mortals staring up, while we are standing down?

-A good life came and went and this and that destroyed the other.-

Finally when he looked upon the rest, he sadly said that we may never go, just beyond the crest,
of this freshly corniced snow.

        Remarks of nonchalance. No fluffer questions. I descended. I failed to know what was after death. If there was nothing, then death would certainly stop me from finding out I was wrong, so even my ego would remain intact. Now what? What to bring along while observing and admiring the sublime idiosyncrasies of my perceived earth? Smiling tears in the eyes. My whole life I had tried to see that void, and just recently along the way I forgot myself at a resting place, what a fool. I was terrified. Self-preservation and perseverance for the love of one's self, one's intellectual evolution, a good state of living. I grabbed some as I walked down and knew some good things about the world. Truth, I think, I must admit, we are but the bold freak, ever changing. Nothing realized is set in stone, only when storms come do we know the response of the ships. All of these accidental classes meant nothing, only over time could I see the truths exposed. I may die never living all of them. When the sun was no longer I walked into the warm room smelling of fire and sandalwood. Sitender and Minori were sitting, sharing stories with faces like children.

Nothing. Nothing. Nearly numb and nodding. All, it is all dearly before us, dumb and simply jotting, notes of this and that as we run on

throughout the middle, god damn it I shall now stop to ask the writer
who sits to type and twiddle.

       Together we descended in the early morning. The trail went easy, we didn't speak. Sitender and I gave our farewells to Minori, exchanging long nods. Minori's wool sweatshirt smelled of dew and flowers. We waved as his face disappeared into the rearview mirror. The ambulance putted along down the road. Once more we stopped at the gorge and hung our bodies over its walls falling to the river. A moment beyond fearlessness of death. We kept on down until we found a good rest house for the night. An elderly woman greeted us and led us through a dining hall where a few silent pilgrims sat eating. She gave us a room facing the Ganga. Outside I sat beside the road on a white wooden chair. Two walking pilgrims approached me. I sat with them speaking of the nature of being. One of the men was sure that we did not exist at all, that we are and see mere imaginations we perceive. The other man was less sure, he made it clear he thought whatever it is that are guilty of being, it is incomprehensible to us. I walked off to see what Sitender was doing. He had been around the ambulance with a confused expression. He told me that we should clean the ambulance, that way it could be beautiful and then we too could be beautiful along with it in the morning after we bathed. A wonderful idea. We took the ambulance to a nearby water pump and took turns pumping water into a metal basin. Some children came by and helped us wash. We threw water on one another. I had lost all of whatever I thought I had, I had stared at the world and I wasn't sure what to think of it. It was beautiful the way flowers were only because they died. Important the way people were because they were only you and I and noble like war for its pursuits of peace. I fell asleep to the cold air on my face and the smell I could never rightly explain of the Himalayas. The radio had run out of batteries so it was silent. By evening next day we would be back in Ghadughat.

Most of these things for which we worry never rise to fruition

Yet these worries for the worried halt my ears to stop and listen

My birthday, the day on which I had become an animal, came while in Ghadughat. I spent the time alone in the hills. My previous birthday I spent in a long-distance coach bus traveling through Chile. A man sitting next to me discovered it was my birthday and demanded the rest of the passengers sing in my honor. We drank a bit and sang more songs after that into the night. This year was silent. The significance of age and experience, and then the irrelevance of both. I was looking down at my whitewashed cottage in the midst of browning fields. Monsoon was late and the whole place seemed drowsy. A thought came to mind, temporary revelations; a group of tantric priests now lived on the land, they were performing fire ceremonies to remove the negative energies of the land. Their company was dark, they drank copious amounts becoming demented, a barbaric ritual ground. Maybe I should take rest, rest for my mind, I thought. Maybe I should write more, write for a while, some more poetry. To the Andaman Islands, an archipelago in the Bay of Bengal. I had to go. I'll leave now, I said aloud.

The madness of war. John Smith. Let us build you a bridge and give you healthcare. I dare you to decline. The pointless fight along this man-made line. Develop. Rely. Rewind.

I packed away my belongings from the room beside the Riba. A calendar hung above my bed. I marked off the days one by one when I first arrived but stopped after some days and just forgot about the time. It was the last thing I removed; a bare white wall was left behind. With my belongings together I sat on the front steps, made a tea, and looked all around. I already missed the town, the familiarity. I wanted to thank the people I had met; they could never know, no matter how minute, that I might see it then or maybe I would really see it in twenty years. It was Sadar with his wife and family, the Swiss man that held his eccentricities high, humble Rawat, and of course the others. I started for town through the waterways. With each person I had a Chi, and with each person was said something of good passing like it always was. I spent the evening at Sitender's, we danced together and cooked over an open fire. Beautiful illusions. Truths from what we know.

Flowers before the peaking sillies sick with laughter.
And all those god damn millionaires wandering round the desert.
The human stoop stuck in satire.

Chocolate cake is for dessert.

The floor was shiny. A good guesthouse by the good piece of beach in town, close to the bridge. I had arranged to stay there for the evening before training to Delhi, to give the town some time. I sat on the balcony low by the twirling waters. Cool tiles under my feet. The "Happy Rishikesh" song played from a deck nearby. I heard it there before, so I leaned back in my chair and smiled up towards the blue. The river turned and made sounds of swashing, birds flew round. The aroma of all of us meeting the sun and rain, with soul, soil, and spice. It was all so great and terrible at the same time. Such a world of love and the children of people searching around all here for no reason at all and for the greatest reason there is. I cried deeply into my hands. Like a beggar for mercy I wished only to be satisfied with all the others. I want to be happy, I cried to myself. What is it in me that wishes such vast constructions? I sipped a lassie with Bhupi, over at shop he showed me to when we had first met. He'd recovered from Jaundice a week or so before. He looked sad that I was leaving. "Why are you going, Prem G?" he asked softly."I have to go, Bhupi."Bhupi laughed. "Yes, you have to go. You go, you go and enjoy, there's nothing else to it.""I wouldn't think of doing anything else, and Bhupi you're such a good man, always a good man." We sipped lassies, then Bhupi and I parted ways with a smile. I walked away triumphant. Bhupi was a good friend. He asked for nothing and started with a smile.
I purchased a ticket in town, my father was kind enough to fund a flight to the islands for reasons he was unaware of. The next day I would leave. Fast like that. It was my last swim in the Ganga that seemed most irrelevant. I suppose I tried not to make it feel final by making it menial. I will go back again, so with this I felt I should leave as if I may return the next day.

I sat on the stairs below the guesthouse leading into the water, my feet cooled below the current. Crowds walked across the bridge in the distance. I was lonely. I had not found success alone, happiness alone. My mind gave me reasons to leave. There was no reason to leave anyplace. I was leaving anyhow, and I knew it then and there. I went back to my room and had my first sleepless night.

With morning I made my way to the cafe across the way for some writing. I had been inspired to write a letter to Swami G, I felt I had to let him know how I saw him. With fury and hate I lashed words together to make an awful letter. Denouncing Bhodi and his monasticism, I wrote of his hypocrisy towards sexuality and his fondness for young boys and pornography. I described the breach of trust I had experienced in his company. I informed him of the robbery in a way that seemed deserving and just. Out of my mind I wrote, for reasons unknown. Building scarecrows to save the birds. No problems in my mind. I had a tea and watched the bridge. I packed my things together back at the room, walked the bridge a last time, and found a rickshaw driver I had used before. Driving out of town down the road I passed the sign again: Do good, be good.

I feel I've wasted time, no. Damn it all to the basement of my head.
A furious feeling.
My heart is thumping as I smoke this one last thought.
Goodbye cliché hunting, goodbye Ghadughat. .

Island Excessum

Chapter Eight

        Death cards from the Tarot present us change; the death is implicit of birth. I boarded the plane heading for the islands, I took a neat whisky with two cubes and a clove back with affluence. The ancient ethic of man never having enough, back from when we lived in the dangerous jungles. I read and write of the ego; we write why we desire not what we have but what we lack, our interpreted identity, desires from sex or depression or this and that. As I watched myself thought, Mental freedom evades me with all these imagined dimensional distinctions. Who is this that cannot differentiate the mind noise from reality and all the other things? We flew over the islands.

This purple blue breeze island implies my will's intention.
Sweet Rhine dunes flutter off prose to over dined dimensions.
Freak of vision, layers of view. A sweet ascension as the purple breeze comes blue.

        A ferry took me from the main island to the island of H. I was the only tourist at the time. It was off-season and hard rain was expected often. A slow ride. I sat out on deck feeling the spray of the waves on my face as they misted over the bow. When shore came to view, feelings arose within me, something like Bojangles, cine, buffalo girls wont you come out tonight, and Rumi. It was all out there, and I was free as any other just wandering to write around.

        The dock led into a simple looking place with jungle fauna and stretches of white beach rolling down into the water azure. I got my paperwork right and hailed a rickshaw to go off looking for a good room. The first resort I checked was a place close to town in the head of the small harbor there. The second was down the road a ways with a handful of bamboo cabanas resting under the shade of palms. Birds. A bit of music. breeze. Out there through the trees. White to blue. A man in white and green Cotton came out to greet me. He introduced himself as Ali. Ali was with a fresh smile and doe eyes, a good man. The company of good men is worth a lot. Ali showed me around giggling; he informed me that I was the only guest and that if I wanted, I could take the biggest room for the price of the smallest. Only if people came would I have to move to a smaller room. Ali was a man like that, nothing trivial, but everything trivial. I unpacked my things in the two-story cabana and sat in a wicker chair up on the porch. There I breathed long slow breaths, looking out onto the coral beneath the calm water and the sand crawling along.

The city turns and tightly talks for royal treatments fit for kings that kings need not pay envy.
The city burns yet still we gawk at royal treatments fit for kings that cost us not one penny.

        Just beyond the trees walks a slender body with a familiar face. Yael, the sharp tapering beam of a woman I met north in the Ganga. She walked along the sand, a yellow shawl wrapped around her waist. I slid across the courtyard and joined her stride. "Yael," I said softly."Prem, " she said, spoken as if this meeting was an eventuality, the flutter of dimensions. "Life, Yael, just like this." We laughed. "Yes, just like this." Why like this? I wondered.We walked along the beach with our hands gently in one another's. Life, like momentary bouts of victory, triumphant walks with thoughtless movements. Finally peace comes, and then gone again like hummingbirds to a sweet flower. We went up and down the beach. We spoke of something I could not even write with a stumbling mumble, it's simply useless. She left off towards the end of the beach to meet some friends she had with her. I let her go and walked along for a swim on down the way.

        In my wicker chair I wrote. I wrote a poem that seems to speak curiously of my disappointed self, from the standpoint of my glorified self. It was a work in progress when a voice called my name from below the balcony. It was Rama, the child worker of the place; he knew my name from Ali, and although still young had a perfectly night-black mustache with the rest of his face pristine and smooth. He called me over to the dining area where Ali sat smoking a cigarette. We sat down together. Ali looked at me smiling, smiling hard, like he held a freedom that drew too much debt to create. He looked at me in the eyes, "I want to know for what reason, because I am especially curious of you young travelers and how they came to be here, and want to ask you if you do not mind, of course, you are here?" He sat back and took a drag of his cigarette. "I am doing my best, Ali." I laughed. Ali and Rama did as well. "Yes, Prem, we're all doing our best, but otherwise, tell me, please, what may you be doing here with us?" Again, over and over. Are we doing nothing here? It would be heartless to see the truth and kill it only because it had died among the others. "Ali, I know what you'd like to know, and the truth is in a short flow, as if we become what we run from and despise, the twisting fates. I must have seen myself as what I thought myself to be, only just recently have I begun to see what I really am, not what I think. I am here now, I suppose, to reflect on these subjects. That is what I am doing here, Ali, looking for these things that must not be looked for." After this monologue, Ali sat back and sighed. "The words you know, but this is beautiful, I met you just today and feel as we know each other very well. I trust you with my words, I see that you have given me your heart after a mere request, this is love. Tomorrow I'll tell you what I'm doing here." We spoke a little about the island into the evening. Fresh barracuda caught that afternoon found its way to my plate for dinner. Sleep in the night was as natural as being awake, the two mixed together seamlessly.

I awoke with the sun coming through the walls weaved from husk. With some shorts, I made my way down towards the beach. I swam off the land into the warm water and let the day come and wake me as I floated on my back. Not too far down the road a farmhouse with a bike shack in the front doubled as a shop, an old man sitting inside on a low stool. I rented a green cruiser for the week and rode off towards a stretch of beach Ali had told me about. For the journey I had with me some rupees, a notebook, and a pen. Through the fields of rice with the wind over my ears. On the other end of the island I parked my bike near a group of shops. A coconut vendor was there so I bought a fresh one for the milk and tender meat. I left the bike by a tree and started along the beach.

After a ways wrapping around the coastline, I came to the center of a crest forming a type of lagoon where I sat beneath a palm and wrote. I begin to write a story about a couple living in an apartment building in New York City, a strange thing to write in such a setting. It was a stream of consciousness piece or something like that. It reflected on the people I had met in India and some other people I saw as pure character; those people were living in the apartment building with the couple, which was me and a girl from pure imagination. What a special girl. I even included a dealer of grass I knew fairly well during high school. He was a good guy and I always saw him as the definition of a character, he was the definition of his mood. After too many pages I became sick with the story and jettisoned the idea of completing it. A waste, I thought, I should write about something more personal. I went on with some free-flowing somethings and read them back to myself repeating each line twice with a raspy voice as to make it sound deep and important. The Bay of Bengal was my crowd and the beach my stage.

Douse me in the fire of these oceans.
Drink suns from the palm of your sky.
Dance in her arms till you tire below them.
Dibbling dabbling crayoned with my.
He's renounced serving moods of plural time; as the blue comes white -
Subject sky.

With the evening I was back at the resort. Ali was there with Rama and the other boys, and they sat at the table speaking of the true aspects of love. Rama looked to get married to a young girl on the island. The other boys poked fun at him but Ali made sure they took the matter seriously. I sat with them and listened. The abstract nature of love so complex in its way may never be understood by man. Affection or attachment, Platonic or chemical, religious or romantic, all are love, for love is, but it's so difficult what the masses decide upon, the confused majority, when we listen not to our hearts but to our useless minds. As he promised, Ali ended the discussion of love shortly after I arrived and began describing why he was there on the island. It turned out that he was from the mainland, Calcutta. Most of the people who were not born on the islands were migrants from Calcutta. Ali's family still lived there; he saw them only once a year during his allotted break. The job he had was the best he could find, and the life he led the best he could lead, so he took it to support his family, raise them in wealth and live in peace. He missed them dearly but said he was there for what he figured duty to be. A lesson, to be without his family. His eyes watered describing this and I could see Ali was a soft man who gave love easily and received love in droves, but lost his true heart to melancholy.

Later when the sun was all gone, I met with Yael. I was writing, sprawled out on a hammock that hung beneath an old low-lying mangrove bent seaward from the wind. I had a feeling she would cross there. She came up and sat at my side with her back towards me. She watched the rippling stars in the water and told me there would soon be a solar eclipse one morning just after sun rise. We lay together and I drew light circles on her lower back, and as I stared around at the heaven to which I had come and figuratively purposed, I resigned further to care nothing for the trivialities like inside-out or outside-in, personal revolutions, temporary hatreds, and mirage epiphanies. It is part and parcel that the arrogance within me initially drove me to find these points, so I thank the wild partial personas of which we are all guilty of sheltering within. It is my journey after all, and it is only truth that these things I felt then did not exist in my ways before, to alter, to be company of exchange, the audience of progression comfortably sitting noplace. Yael turned and looked me in the eyes. "Wondrous places simply don't matter without good company, isn't it so?" Something like this, you know. And was it her who made me feel this way? It is not so, everything and anything you could think of helps me to arrive each time around. We ran across the beach for a nude bath in the moonlit water, making love in the sand, alive and with moving sounds of static. Who wins? We all do; you.

Yael went on her way, back to the mainland someplace. The last time I saw her we pointed to each other on the beach, smiling with our arms out stretched forward. I never saw her again, this wonderful woman, who might have been dreams. So I went on about the island. I drank because it seemed the best thing to do. Posture seemed stupid and archaic. I spoke with Ali and the boys every night about whatever we had on our minds, but they could not understand me. I read more. I drank. I passed out and lost the ability to write. I took to reorganizing the resort library. I felt good. I have read some of these, I would think. From a collection of a few hundred books in all different languages, I found a good few and read them over. *The Koan Tiki Expedition* made me think seaward. I thought maybe I should sail across the open sea and let my life be taken in the hands of chance in the fluids of earth. I read over *A Tale of Two Cities* and it seemed to be the best of books and the worst of books. I read Hemmingway and he made me drink more. I went on again with Tolstoy, again *Father Sergius*. The idealized heaven; limbo in paradise.

Adoration of the histories that by chance we don't receive.
Intonations of preambles that we dance but won't believe.
He is Paris, he is Russia, he is forest, he is tree.
If only he could know that it is them who we do be.

A young Englishman, like a liberal hooligan, came to the island and stayed in a cabana. I moved to a smaller one. We had a smoke upon our first meeting. He was a rough guy and I didn't take to him so I cut our meeting short and biked off to where I regularly took lunch at a small tali place in the center of town. It was right beside the vegetable market where all the locals gathered. I saw a few more tourist around, they went on about their ways. What were they doing, I wondered, what was their story. I go spatial.

Early morning I walked along the beach. A local fisherman gathered his gear. He wore neon green short-shorts and had black curly hair. In his right hand was a metal barbed spear and in the other two lobsters. I was amused by him, as he was with me. I was wearing a Technicolor dhoti and in my hand was a white flower. He spoke no English but I managed to get across that I wanted to purchase a spear like the one he had. He understood and motioned that he would return the next day.

Ali helped barter the deal, so I got myself the spear. The hunt. With my acquired tool and goggles in hand I rode off towards the beach on the other side of the island. As I walked the white sands I crossed the path of a Frenchman who was wandering around there. He had a smoke with him and shared it with me as we sat on the sand; we exchanged only nods. I kept on and made it to a good point of shallow water with healthy reef below. I swam out with the spear and began trying different techniques of thrusting. I feel a whole lot better about eating animals that I myself have killed, there's something about it. I found a good technique and floated, waiting for fish to come. I got a chance to spear one, my aim disturbed by a fault in form. The rubber band took some time to master. I took it and missed. The water was still while waiting for the fish to come. This day I caught nothing. As I rode back to the cabanas a young boy from the island came up beside me and offered to race; we pedaled fast all through the rice fields and past the huts and people, and we both threw up our arms in a dance as we rode into town, hooray.

I got beers with the Englishman in the evening. He was an odd fellow. It seemed like he was minutely angry with everything, even the beer. That evening before sleep I read and re-read Rumi's *Night and Sleep*. I desired to harvest dreams, I dreamt that man offered me the power of turquoise once, I didn't know how to take it. Then the possible lucid dreaming. It was not always so, but when it did happen it brought a great satisfaction when I awoke in the morning, at ease with all the other things.

When I went to check my networks to the west for the first time on the island I received a letter from Bhodi. I saw it had been copied to my mother and father. The letter was entitled, "your criminal activity,", As I sat in the cold computer booth designed retro in a wet white bathing suit and a purple flower shirt, I wondered what it was about. A calamity of worth I laughed, Bhodi had lost the idea to his only rule, reaction. The letter stated that I had stolen the money entrusted to me in the north and that I had been doing hard drugs and drinking daily in Ghadughat. It even stated that I stole the ambulance to joyride around the mountains. He also wrote that if I did not return the money within a few weeks he would contact the police. Who knows what he wanted to tell them. He stated that I would be unable to leave the country. After reading this I felt an empty feeling in my stomach. Look at this, I laughed, trouble in paradise. My parents were obviously concerned by this. I had no control over what they thought about it, the letter was written two weeks before so it had time to ferment in the mind of curious parties without my rebuttal. I took it, a wrongdoing in the book, something else in the moment, but we live with our decisions. It felt good at the time. What is all of this anyway? I left the computer and went outside. I twiddled my thumbs and remembered those musical pilgrim lawyers I had sat with in the back of that truck. One of their cards remained in my wallet.

I called the number with a pay phone. A man answered. He knew it was me the second I spoke. He laughed and asked if I was in prison or something of that nature. I informed him of my dilemma. He let me know my predicament was containable, that the amount of money that I was accused of stealing was not a federal problem and I was out of state. Still, Bhodi could tell the police anything. He told me to stay where I was and to relax, and to maybe write a positive letter in a few days time. I thanked him and knew the week would be busy with unimportant talks and explanations. A fool's errand.

Go fetch these things you said until these days run dry.
Protect the whims you bed to spill these teaming tinctured tides.
She pokes the rosy red petals- that now wilt to the side.
These airs strikes her eyes and the minds begins to slide.
On and on this stare hikes sky as these minds lag behind.

A liar I had become. The perils of Robin Hood, born from the egoistic Utopian move. The paradoxical dictator of Eden, the liar, the fool of imagined wealth. Who is to be in charge of love? But I knew I had not stolen the money in my heart of hearts, so I told my parents that I hadn't. I sat with Ali back at the resort cafe. He thought my situation was something of a comedy. I thought about it. Bhodi resented me for putting his cards on the table. I carelessly confronted him about his bad character. All before heisting his loot in the name of some self-implied goodness with a cartoon explanation. I stole from him. What have I done? I thought. But I can do nothing. What have we all done. Bhodi was not a bad man, merely running and confused, and who was I to bask in projections, it seemed I was doing the same.

There are no rules, paradigms, names, nor any words . No up or a
down. Not a smile nor a frown. You are rule. With not a square or one
round. The king; the effervescent lips of the one beyond these bending
sheets.

I lay writing in the hammock watching the beach. In the distance "Oreo Cookie Blues" played from the old cafe speakers. Poetry, poetry is as much for me as the people I may read it to, or is writing useless for one's self, as all the writing one could ever do is already within one's mind. Is it only the outsiders who need understand us? But poetry, poetry is the game of words, the manipulation of

useless words to promote abstract feelings to arise within the mind.
Powerful thrust in the stone. These games of words surprise me, I have
read one poem the length of my hand so well written that I might not
even hope to project a morsel of its meaning within all of the words of
this entire book. I have so much time to think, this is a good place to
think, I thought. A group of Germans came into the resort. I watched
them as they chose their cabanas around the grounds. It was me the
Englishman and now five German women. The place would be more
lively. I did prefer to be alone, but didn't see a difference.

In the evening I made way into the cafe. Guests gathered by a
large low-lying table set up on a wooden platform, and cushions lined
the floor. Booze and bags of grass were out and I joined them. The
Englishman and the Germans were sitting; one of them taught me the
Greek alphabet. Does Obama just love his father, it is all the inner
satisfaction of resolute production, is that why he's the president, and
we all laughed at one another playing drinking games. A young
Canadian came with a guitar and two long chains with torches attached
at the ends. We sang the songs of freedom and watched him calmly
swing fire beneath the moon. As the night grew older each person made
his way off to bed, the air warm from the day and the stars brilliant in
the clear sky. I was left at the table alongside another. We went for a
swim, leaving our cloths on the beach and walking out onto the wet
sand. The tide was going out and some reef peeked out from the water.
Wet sand went far out off the beach. We walked out, stars reflected in
puddles. We swam out into the shallow and floated on our backs. The
stars, more stars than black. Naked under the cosmos, floating in this
resting water, I was pointless and infinitely insignificant yet profound
as the lens with which I viewed the night sky. Solar eclipse.

It has all come down. I look up as the rest in these histories of
invariable movement through and through sparkled and cast. This
word came from this place. It all seems very familiar.

I spoke little with the Germans after that first time, as well as
the Englishman and the Canadian. I spoke with Ali sometimes, but kept
on to myself, writing and walking around the island. My father out of
fear for my safety paid Bhodi the money he accused me of stealing. I
was ashamed for cultivating such an episode. I'll pay him back with the
proceeds of this book. He will understand as I suppose all the others

will. The nature of class. After receiving a dark letter from Bhodi explaining my psychotic state, I contemplated telling them what had happened but chose passive timelessness. I felt an alienated feeling, the feeling I got when I was a young boy, when all the people around me simply thought I was not like them and could not possibly become so, the stigma of it all made me equally as crazy as they imagined me to be. Yell at me for crying until I cry, then you will see I'll cry all day. It was kamikaze. I fell to my knees in the woods walking back from spear-fishing, I had lost my way and cried for everything I knew about myself. Set them free, I lost you, you lost yourself, but maybe I was glad to be rid of them.

By the end of my stay on the island I had done nothing significant. Reading. Failed silence. Booze. Smoke. Polluted thoughts and stolen moments. For money I went back and forth a few times from the mainland to the island of H with bottles of rum to sell to the tourists and locals, as the island was dry at that time of the off-season. Even with this extra money I found myself broke by the end, unable to pay the bill. My father bailed me out without question, and I was grateful. And I despised my thought for gold idea and dream. My break seemed over. My stories and poems seemed compromised, the drama had a larger effect on me than I saw. I had to be getting back to the mainland, so I booked a cot on a freighter to be on my way. Ali walked me to the dock where the ferry was waiting. He stood and explained to me, " You young men have all the reason you could ever want, so don't stop walking round until you've found the right spot to think about it." Ali cried, he truly gave his love without question. I was the fleeting youth of Ali. All the while it rained only thrice.

Yo-yo man,
The old world is dead.
Give it here.

The freighter to Chennai back on the mainland was simple. It was an uneventful ride but a stupor into future stole me. My journey seemed tainted. I fermented on the negative side. How stupid of me to go along with my optimistic compulsions, I thought, giving in to my imagined happiness. What is real happiness? In the deep of my heart I saw that places didn't mean a thing to interpreted happiness, yet I kept going on and couldn't figure why. I feel that one must fall to rise, and one must be ready to fall, not a woman nor money or status could change the sick feeling that arose within my stomach. A self of lies for the projection is off-color. If there is nothing more than this, as I feel, why do I feel so empty this way, alone to long for my own good, self-exiling myself from concrete human interactions. But it has been so all along, I fear. No difference. I tore to pieces a notebook my hand filled with poems from the other place. A loud anger chased after the honesty I held with myself.

Lapping, turning, rolling tunes swish. I patiently sit in this waiting rooms stitch.

I arrived in the dusty smoke-topped Chennai late in the evening and made my way into a busy part of town in the textile district. I got a room for the price of a few cigarettes and fell asleep looking up towards the ceiling of chipping lead paint, the home smell of mold and bidis all around. I dreamed the northern hills, the beggar of joy. Beyond absurd torture, our involuntary movements, forgivable, our inability to run from things that we know to be fatal, institutionalism ends and the hearts wind wins back the sail. And all the same. The dream, and I awoke happy wondering where I was.

As its malevolent behavior increased beyond my teeth.
That day diligent doppelganger deceased beneath my feet.
He tried to kill the cast and cause them all neurosis;
Instead he chose to coddle last the lovelies made for lonelies.

I was in Chennai and it was just after sunrise. I walked down from the old hostel for some breakfast. I ate alone in silence. I saw other westerners but felt it best not to speak with anyone unless they spoke with me. I didn't want to take the chance of changing my fate by disturbing it with meaningless conversations that I would have to sincerely invent to begin in the first place. There was nothing on my mind for talk except maybe the weather. After breakfast I walked around the city streets brimming with people. Above a sweet shop and up some crumbling stairs I entered into an old office that was directly across from a room full of men sitting cross-legged sewing leather sandals together. In the office a woman in a burka greeted me in silence and showed me to a chair. I sat and she placed a cup of tea on a table beside me. A man came in, he was at my service at once; he got me a good ticket over to Kerala the following afternoon. A simple terminal on the second story of noplace that could sell me a ticket to anyplace I wished to go. We finished the business. He smiled and pointed to a pitch dark back room. I walked back. I walked in. It smelled of sawdust. In the center of the room where I felt around for a sofa chair, I sat. The door closed behind me, only a few small led lights could be seen around, and at once a stream of the most filling sounds found their way into my head, the entire room was filled from top to bottom with custom speakers, walls of sound. A room of sound up in that crumbling building.

BOOM. Swash, the deep sounds of bass and others having fun. So good, the best sounds I had ever heard. Love, I thought, what else would it be. He turned on the lights and opened the door. The man laughed. "Thought I maybe was going to kill you, huh? It looked as if you may have needed some top sound in your life." Yes, top sound. I thanked him. "We are only as good as how we treat strangers in our lives, aren't we? You're young, you've got time to learn this, so listen to the sounds and smile often." I handed him a ring off my finger that I purchased in Nepal, a cheap piece but it meant a lot. I gave him a smile. "Top sound for you," I said. The man laughed. We exchanged nods and I made my way back towards the hall leading down the stairs and out to the street.

When the evening came I had a feathery swagger to my walk. I felt the people in the streets as I had not before. No reason or end. I could do nothing for them, I had little money and my hands were weaker than most of theirs. I consoled myself to think I was here to learn as much about the way they lived and how they felt and saw content and beauty. For me to help anyone I would first have to help myself, to bring this place along with me. As I was walked the streets at a late hour feeling this way, thinking of these things, three street guys stared me down with their big dark eyes. They wore cheap dress shirts with bright colors and their arms were big and inflexible like gorillas. I passed and they smelled of liquor. They looked and I nodded cordially, and kept walking. A few yards down one of them called after me, "American! Hey you, American! Come talk with us famous men." Trouble comes and you can always feel it coming like weightless steps. I'll have to kill these fuckers, I thought. I left walking around a corner. I looked around and found a steel reinforcement bar the length of my arm and grabbed it, putting it in my pants. I heard them coming after me laughing to one another. When I began walking faster they ran after me and circled around. I thought about it and concluded it would be a better choice to give them what I had than to get into a fight. The smallest one put out his hand and yelled that I give him all my shit. I handed him the wallet, he looked inside unsatisfied. Another one removed a knife, and in a moment they advanced. On second thought, I thought, fuck them. I turned and quickly removed the bar and swiped the guy with the wallet in the neck. A gash opened, he held up his hands, he dropped the wallet and began screaming and moaning, cursing for the others. They stepped back in a fighting stance.

The both of them come at me. I hit the one with the blade as hard as I could on the knuckles and tore his hand wide open. The other came at me and jabbed me in the stomach. I stumbled back, and he ran up and got me in the face. I ran back and regained my ground. The smallest was still on the ground. I began screaming as a wild animal might, hitting the bar on a poll beside me. My nose bled down my face and my lip cut below. The two men standing looked at me with a strange accordance. They lifted the other one and ran off into the night. I got my wallet from off the ground. I laughed hysterically in the street, and then tears came. Those people could not be my friends and it shamed me. I walked back to the hostel as steady as I could. I didn't find sleep that night. In the collection fluttered the absurdities of human culture, fighting one another on the street, bureaucratic systems working all over the world to keep people starving and places dirty. The blood for blood. We have not changed. The relief, there are no remedies here. Catharsis Americana.

He may never find her more, for through his door he let her slip. She told him it was a high that he was after but he swore it wasn't so. It was a place he yearned to live. Life without these rooms, indifferent to the contemporaneous natures of laws without one bloom. These lines they do not lead, but hunch and slowly follow, march and quickly chase. He so dearly wants to play with them but none are set with tokens. He chuckles with his one last coin with string attached within, so he plays a thousand songs on the joke box, for all those standing next to him.

Light Sounds Different

Chapter Nine

Kerala was a beach place on the Arabian Sea. I stayed in a town by the name of V. And as I walked from the rickshaw that had taken me from the station, I jealously breathed familiar air from over the red cliffs. I was just moving along with a thought of women. To shelter my mind and body a good hostel was in order, and back a ways from the main street I found one. A Sikh man by the name of Akbar ran the place. He was young and chubby but had something to him. His beard was partly grayed. I got a room on the ground floor with a patio, but knew little time would be spent within the confines of its walls.

The fading cross to wave the tumbles
Find her in these wading rumbles
Through the fading wave that crumbles
Find here in these something symbols
The ending start of sounds to jumble

I swam in the ocean. I swam far out past the break and floated on my back and lost sight of things. I lost sight of things out there in the surf, and when I came back I saw that the current had swept me past down the beach off a pointing bluff. Waves crashed towards sea-beaten rocks. I roll with the waves and slowly make my way from out of current. I slithered my way across. I lay on the beach front a ways down beside an open cafe wondering why I had not let the ocean sweep me to where it had wanted. Music ran through me, that special tingling treble arousal.

A Spaniard from a table in the sand called me over; she was with what looked to be her partner. I walked to them, and they pointed to an empty seat. They demanded through white smiling teeth that I share with them mojitos. They thought it silly for me to be alone in the sun without a beverage or company.

This stoned couple from Majorca were in their twenties. We spoke of contemporary education while I chewed bits of mint. The retention of regurgitated material is of no dire importance, but rather the conceptualization of abstract ideas and the ability to seamlessly adapt to various situations, for with this we can become everyone. Imagine a world where people only knew what they knew to get someplace. I wondered if we were there. Knowledge is more than a vessel for travel and material gain. It wouldn't matter what you knew, it would only matter how you came to know it and what could be done with it. We didn't exactly know what we were talking about, but it was clear that the three of us had hard feeling towards non-interactive schooling environments with multiple choice and strawberry milk served in cardboard cartons. I left the couple and started back to my room for a nap.

It was late that night I awoke, but an urge to dance came to mind. I started for the front desk to see if Akbar wanted to spend the evening in the streets. Of course he did, so we went off for the opening of a club on the cliffside. I felt good, but I felt out of place. I had not done the club scene in a while, and it seemed to be a fair contrast. We got a table amidst the loud music. An Italian girl with a tattoo of bamboo flowing down her shoulder sat down at the table with us, she was with a guy but he didn't seem important. We exchange ideas. I lit a spliff and passed it round. I sat and watched the people dance for a good while. I left from the table for a smoke along the cliffside. An old German rocker left back from the sixties went on about how people are inherently good and we are all pure at heart, it is only evil that tempts us to stray from ourselves. This evil is the man in the room who wants to be someplace else, the evil is the feeling you get when you are lonely and it is the candy you will not refuse. I listened to him and enjoyed the ideas; he was a free man and an old one at that, a rare find. He held out his hand and gave me a child-minding wink, I held out my own in reception, and carefully he placed a tab of LSD into my palm. He smiled and shrugged his shoulders. Without a word I rested the tab atop my tongue and let it be. The whim. I thanked the German with a crazy laughter and motioned for us to return back to the table.

Some others were their but I was caught by Akbar. He was depressed, the expression he wore looked as if he was bored with everything. I offered my ear in conversation. The drug hadn't come to mind. We spoke and I learned that Akbar was from Sri Lanka, he had rented his hostel with monetary help from his parents. It seemed as though something had happened to make him leave his home. What was his purpose? I had none at all. The feeling of change came, the temperature and the simple perceptions went wonder-working. "I don't understand this place," Akbar said with passion. I laughed. "I don't either, Akbar. I'd say A lot of people have told me a lot of things, a lot of people have done a lot of things to prove a lot of things, but there's nothing to understand." He looked at me as if he knew what I said to be true but couldn't find it in his day. "Have you heard of tsunamis?" he asked disconcertingly. "Yes, Akbar, yes I have." "Let me tell you something, OK. Do you want to hear something?" "Of course.""I lived in Sri Lanka a while before, you see. When the waves came a few years ago I was there. It was just a normal day, a normal day I was walking around the beach when the water started coming down. All the locals went to the beach looking at the low tide. They should have known, the native Indians did, but that knowledge is dead to us. Then the water came way up onto the beach and then went back down again. I ran for my house to tell my friends after that first rise. While I was in the courtyard, water came up, more and more water, a ton of it. I don't remember much else. My mind went into a survival mode of sorts, or maybe a paralysis or something. Only in flashes do I remember. There I was hanging on and saw people dead, friends and people I knew from the streets, but it seemed like it was a normal day with the sun bright in the sky. I walked around confused and nothing made sense. I got depressed after, really. I don't know what to make of anything, so I'm running this hostel over here for a little while.

"Listening, I had been looking over the cliffs into the breaking waves. When a wave came it would crest with a blue silver lining then crash into a purple mist. I was speechless when I looked for a response. I could only find, "An amazing happening, Akbar, you are." He was interested in his own courage to describe his experience; I was not important. "I don't know, maybe I saw life one way before and now I see it differently, so it's like being a child all over again trying to make sense of even the simple things." "All are with a different blue.""Yeah.""It is only calm when we are together in mind."" Your eyes, your eyes look big and your smiling. You're high, huh?" Yeah, a bit." "What have you got? I've got a nice hash here."
"Some LSD, Akbar, that is what I have done."
"What is it like?" The conversation we had held seemed over once this was mentioned, so I left it alone. I wanted to know more, more of how we change from one way to the next. Do we only perceive ourselves differently over time, is that what changes? I am truly a mess now and

then. "It's something you have to experience to know, it's like seeing what you've never cared to notice and it's the truth if we can find it and the lie if we believe. "Akbar laughed, and I did as well when I pondered my own free words. "You got any more? I could join you in the freedom." "No, I got it from the retro guy, the one with the gray braids."The whole club disappeared and I found myself in a different place, thinking. Time had always been, and everything seemed to be destroyed by time, but it was because of time that water quenched my thirst. Pure expression in the sense it had become this way, slowly over time, free from the ideas of anything and everything in every bit of existence. I made my way onto the beach, it was red and when the water came up upon dry sand at the zenith of its reach it danced back down quickly with the light fading behind. I walked with the wind, I was the beaches and hills, rivers and oceans. It was as if I were the only one on the planet and not a morsel of fear existed within me, the earth was loud with no voices, the beach was slow and I walked as if I were in a blizzard.

Akbar came and he amused me, he was eyes-dancing happy and content. No bursts of doubt were suffered, we had grip on perpetual bliss, defeating the mind. Yet it was real as we could see it, and I knew it, but knew just the same that it was nothing. We wandered the beach looking around. Akbar walked with a deep lunge, singing to himself. And I watched it all witness to this dream while awake and find what's been lost in your mind by your mind from negligence. Just a man, only a man and nothing more, I am man, you are man. The both of us ran round the shore like wild beasts.

When we had made our way back up the cliffs and onto the walkways along the stores and bars, we skipped and sang and paused and witnessed this place of undulations. We were back near the hostel where we sat in wicker chairs eating green oranges in view of the ocean with our faces set into the wind. The sunrise came, kissing the waters, saturating my views. Only smiling passersby from the night disturbed our birth. I awoke a bit up with *the world is you* on my mind. I made my way to a cafe across the road and sat inside a gazebo facing the ocean. The owner of the place came by and placed a chai and some parathas before me. His face resembled Osho, and he had a big belly. He was seriously personable and spoke with such a calculation. Osho crashed Bentleys in the dessert for fun, this is eccentric. This man was the first man I spoke with and he filled me with feelings of truth. We spoke of the meaning of aum, that base line vibe of which all is, comes and goes, comes and goes, the expression of the transformable zero. An idea. I want to know the sound but feared I might never have time to sit and listen. I was the idea. I no longer felt like a character or an actor, my words came without concern. Fuck me, I thought, all the others, if there are even others that are the same, there must be, static, I shall not submit to the silly and almost obligatory constant lifestyles offered up in exchange for life. The nine-to-five bastards run, make money, and then you're dead and you can even be selfish in the process, terrible. Calm yourself child, I should not hate the world for being so.

My next step was undetermined. I thought of losing my mind and cycling across Mongolia into northwestern China, or smoking hash while bouldering the red rocks of Hampi. I had no care of what was next so I rang my father. I did not want to decide. After speaking, I decided to try and meet a man that went by the name of Helicopter Swami. I had no knowledge of this man, only that he had millions of followers down in the south. My father spoke adamantly on his behalf. He had met him one time way back. Maybe if I met this man, my journey might continue less commonplace for the times after or it might satisfy me enough to call it a night. So I left out of Kerala on the train towards Bangalore. I would have to meet him in the city.

I had no reservations for individuals who are defined by their public as holy or enlightened, yet I hold interest to meet someone who has this type of following and personal life, it must change them. As a throne does to a king. A king is a person but great because he is a king, a king because he has the throne. The things we hold and make into how we walk around looking for things to do. I am he who walks upright and twiddles his thumbs. A good walker was outside a cafe before I took off. He was a student from England, and he went on about how well-read he was, having read all the classics. He knew all the authors and titles, most likely he knew the stories, but if he did, did he know the imaginary and or real people he was reading about? Did he love them? Maybe we're all the same and only perceive our reactions to be personal. As I speak of another's identity I question mine, but know it may never be lost. Like all things, stay sound, lemming, and simply see.

Breath my brothers aren't these just dreams

or haven't we been only tripping, gripping, fanciful themes?

These days

Chapter Ten

   This place was in a low part of Bangalore and I saw no reason to travel out. As I paced the room in which I stayed, something of a sad state approached me. I was part of some generation that suffers in thoughtless silence, highly over-stimulated absent minded youth, void of new thoughts spoken, fear. It made no difference to me whether or not I saw him, there was no reason for all this. To be sunshine, the feeling escaped me still. Waiting alone in that room on the third floor of a crumbling building beside a temple and some offices. The city bustled around and smelled of gas and rot. Who was this idolized man I wished to speak with? I handed importance to an image yet knew there was nothing there more than anywhere else. There was everything and it took me everywhere. I wished for this but still did nothing.

Beneath from where the blunders come, I rock and sway with patience.
In the place from where the umber runs, I mock and play on salience.
No more shall the slumber numb. - I rewind forgetful ailments .

   I waited in that room and around and wasted the mind. I did not invite myself for tea. I lost trust for my own good will. I did not believe my role and denied myself the pleasure of moments. A darkness had come over me. Momentary bouts of freedom; thoughts aboriginal.

Swell dreams lovely dreams
  The wake to sleep so slow

   I fell-in more here with the people, sitting, listening to the words of commentators on electronic viewing stimulators to achieve a glimpse of world. The creations spoken past the lips of man, the words of other men, originality lost to the majority, by the majority. Here we went together all the same and whilst we did I could not help but think that we were absent, if you were who I assumed you to be. Faster into the depths of this and that and people's own unfulfilled futures, an epistemological anarchy. Dog apocalypse. I must carry on and watch the hummingbird as it passes across my view of the dolphin out on the Pacific coast, I thought. Just as I watched the helicopter, as it passed across my view of the ship on the horizon.

Before us, the tangible, the synthesized nature we buy with money, the modern green aristocrat, the co2 emissions of a few Google searches roughly equal to that of boiling a pot of tea. The hybrid suburbans. Packaged chips and pre-sliced onions. Help those savage Indians, they're destroying the coral reefs, stop them, change their lives, we have already destroyed ours, their livelihood is ignorant. Look there, another man in trouble. Look here, a man in the wrong. What are you doing? Where?

I was still going noplace and once more nearly lost the will to enlist in all of this. A young man with no formal education, listen on good sir while the bureaucrats speak ill on the subjects of a friendly matter. Held up in grand rooms reading man's texts miles long, even ethics an issue, fucking the same sex, television rules, the trump, collection creation, shouts of the black man posing a threat to ruin our idealized America, the schoolyard. What you have come to see, without a thought of difference.

Look at these powdered men masquerading around to reach that which they desire. Listen to the drunk party when the evil men are killed. Listen to these youth raised by dead children still protecting their castle in the sand right above the waterline. The little existential crisis. Shall I spend a life perfecting life or work? There should be not a difference, I am beyond behind myself and wish only to create an idea tangibly pleasant. Beyond news and story. Jargon from the heart.

Saddened by interest-driven pieces taking over topics of value, I sit in numb waste. All do not have water, nor even food, people are getting raped and maimed, murdered and tortured, burned. The world. You are the neighborhood. But just as well, silly in-depth cycling imaginations. Here we go and argue between ourselves, the world driven by what other people project from their desire to win, it goes. An America fighting its own freedom. What is this, why watch this propaganda of mood? The era is dead. The false ideological social stratosphere that has given rise to the glorified self pitying millionaires, the staunch fatties grabbing money, the gross commentators spewing hormones at the next man, the word slingers pounding on the pursuit of happiness, while the minds of people are stolen by style and money, it is dieing. Happiness: what we speak of by day and what America masturbates to every night in order to sleep. It is all here, friends, slowly fading into the limelight, so we may all pilot planes for minimum wage and be comedians free of charge on YouTube, this perception. A nightmare.

Would Oprah have enjoyed this book, as I have written into the future, would I have gotten on her list if I had gone further, or better, better written, faster, it took me too long and I dry in the suns, less telling and more showing? Yes, that's it, more connected sense. Use a dingbat or something. This is the question, isn't it, isn't this what I care about, my Ferrari, this literati. Have I whored this expression to the lines of popularity and consciously written in a way fit for the others to enjoy? Thoughts extrapolated to words, then to sounds we may hear in our paralyzed minds and chuckle or cry and ponder about, or repeat to another man. This word has no feeling and that feeling has got no word. We are the limbo language. The scoreless story, a good bathroom book you may enjoy while shitting, or maybe on a bus or train or even a plane if you are fortunate enough. Is your ass showing, are you fat? Are you good-looking enough to date the one you seek? Smart enough to acquire the job you desire? The moron of bastards and the liar of speakers. Passing the time until the lights go dim, just lovin' life while out on this whim.

I slowly paced the room on the fourth morning. A timid security guard rapped at my door. "Sir, you are free to meet with the Helicopter Swami this day." Or he was free to meet me, the busy man, busy with business and other things. This morning he had a moment to spare, so I left my room and followed the boy over to the main building to where Helicopter Swami stayed. I was shuffled past a line of people and sent to wait in an office surrounded by men filled with self-importance. Big fears in these men in suits. When they called my name to go upstairs I gave my mind a second thought and wondered what the fuck I was doing there, in India, seeing this man, in life, breathing this air. What a state I was in. I must have lost my mind someplace in the north.

I walked into a big room lined with leather chairs all facing one direction. On the far wall stood statues and photos of the man I so apparently wished to see. The room was silent and smelled of lemons. I looked around, and a long while passed before an elderly man came from behind a grand oak door engraved with stories from the Mahabharata. He motioned for me to come. As I approached the door a family came out; they each had tears in their eyes and smiles on their lips.

A wide-bellied man with a shaved head, big doe eyes, and an orange robe sat in the back center of the room. He waved for me to approach. I prostrated to his feet as was customary. He gave something of a soft satisfactory grunt. He looked at me. We were silent. He laughed. "So you're a mathematician?" he asked.
"No," I replied, "I am nothing, a student.""Yes, good, a student, and what do you want?" he asked, and picked a red grape."Maybe you can tell me, tell me something and we'll see."He looked at me and smiled. "There is a bus that will pass by the gates to this place tomorrow at sunrise. Board that bus and get off at the last stop." I agreed to do what this glorified man told me, gave him a bow, and left the room. Nothing else was said.

Back at the room I wondered if I should run, run for my life to the mountains and slowly die eating nuts and berries, in peace at least. My mind shuts on and felt no love, anger rose to great heights. There was no place to go and no money to spend and I was sick of asking for it, the blood of this money. I lay across the cold leather bed and wondered how I wanted to be dying, as I die each day, should I write until I mastered the production of word on page, should I work as a clown at a traveling carnival and make all laugh until sick, should I work the system and regard myself as a common man, should I race cars and give them a reason to drink? One day I would live on a beach, the difference was none, and what did I desire but only peace, shining rings, smooth starched clothes, and a big house with a beautiful wife that loves to fuck. And something else, I had spent so long alleviating myself from the epic of ego mind, so predictable and sour, but failure, it was this I needed most in the true games of present, to succeed in the battle of the bacteria. I fell into a depression and wished I had not seen the world in the way I had, if only I had not realized the city in the glass ball, only then could I have lived there happily. Now look! I attempt to shake the globe and make it snow, come city, burn with lights and dreams of young, erase us with your monster, move us through our forfeit, and may we all find what we are looking for. My mind escaped. I was tired already, so young to be tired. All night I silently sobbed for this drab bastard world of mine that I seemed to be waiting in, waiting, waiting, waiting, gone. Depression, I thought, this is real depression, but it too shall pass.

He's arranged all those little letters in the wrong form and order But from this deranged placement he grows young as you wilt olderNot your fault, you were told to, and then warned colder, that all things are so as they powder in the mortar, but none the better as we become one with this slumber.

I awoke and started my way across the property to where the bus would come. While walking, that young man who had knocked at my door the day before came to my side and informed me that the bus had gone and left. I could catch another if I hurried down the road. Then I remembered I didn't even know where I was going. I had never troubled to ask. The young man figured that if I was going anywhere, I would most likely be going the "mutt," as he said, a place in the hills a few hours southwest. So he showed me to a van parked in a lot beside the land on which I stayed. Only one man without the knowledge of English sat in the driver seat, I sat in the back and waited for something to happen. When we took off it didn't matter to me where I was going, as long as I was going, going, going, gone.

After a handful of stops the van filled. People boarding along the way looked to be doctors but none of them spoke with me, and I did not speak with them, instead I rested my head against the window and watched the streets move by. Like ending a drunken night in the a.m. watching people going to work wondering why. We left the city and went driving through open plains speckled with red rock. I drifted off to sleep and awoke a good while later as we pulled into the front of a three-story hospital. I must have taken the wrong route, I thought to myself, and laughed aloud. I got out from the van and walked to the nearest man. "If I were to be going someplace, where would it be?" I asked. The man was old and graying, his dhoti was loosely tied, and his fingernails black. "I imagine if you are going someplace, you may be going to the mutt." "Oh, yes, maybe this is where I should be going." I felt like the little bird from that children's book, "Are you my mother?" So I hailed a rickshaw for the ashram in the hills and drove on through small villages supported by the production of rice and ragi, or nachni as some people call it. The place was out in the boonies from Bangalore and had a tiny population. After riding, we arrived at the base of some high hills littered with white boulders, the center one was outfitted with temples, statues, and all sorts of buildings and religious reference. All marble and granite. I took my things and started my way up a long set of stairs. A few beggars came to my Western body and asked for alms. What a life, life-living on those big stairs, I was so close to being jealous of them. I set my things down when I reached the top and rested on a wall with a view of the plains. I could hear singing coming from the temples, voices of children.

A group of kids out from class came to my side. They approached me smiling and huddled around. The eldest spoke for the group. "What is America like, sir, tell us of America," he said shyly. It is a very fast place. Love does not conquer like here. Money and greed devour us, I thought in my mind. My mind, mind you. They looked at me wide-eyed. I hadn't taken into consideration their age, maybe ten through fifteen. I retracted my thought statement and answered, "America is just like here but larger. It is a wonderful place, but I bet if you went you would miss India. They are alike but so different." They looked surprised. "I am trying to find a place to sleep. Do you know where that might be? The youngest pointed to a large white building down on the plains and rested his head in a pillow with his hands to signify sleep. A rest house, maybe I should be going there, I thought. So I thanked the children and made my way back down the stairs and over to the white building where two men sat smoking on the stairs leading into the place. "Room, G?" one of them asked. "Yes, room," I replied. My broken Hindi was useless here, Kannada was the local tongue, a Dravidian language closely related to Urdu, and I knew nothing of it. I mentioned the name of Swami Balaganga, the formal name of the Helicopter Swami, and somehow got across that I was there by his word. They gave me a room free of charge and let me be. I sat alone in the room, a small cot with a sheet and a bathroom with a hose and hole. I lay in bed staring out the windows and fell asleep as it began to drizzle.

I awoke mid-afternoon and the sky was clear. I ventured out

for a walk in the streets, the whole place was empty, out for lunch. I walked a while until I saw a large group of people gathered together in the distance by a bridge. I started closer to see the reason. There on that bridge sat an old man smoking a bidi, I sat down beside him and watched as the gathering of people all sang and prayed together around a goat decorated with paint and ash. A man with a large knife danced around the animal and stopped in the front of it. He swiftly grabbed the nape of the goat's neck and with one motion quickly sawed off the head. The crowd grew rowdy as the blood flowed heavily from the fallen beast. The doer placed the head of the goat atop an altar for prayers to be offered. The crowd slowly dispersed and made preparations for a feast. All the while I sat with this silent old man who smiled and smoked through his few teeth. "How interesting." I left the bridge and started back for my room. It became dreary once more so I read some Rumi.

The next morning I awoke at sunrise to the voices of children outside my door. Curious children looking for my company. I slipped on some clothes and stepped outside. It was the same children from the day before. "Swami G is here today in little time," the eldest said. "Oh, thank you, where can I find him?" "In the evening you go to the main temple, he will sit there later." "Thank you, I will, and, food, where is food?" "You come with us now." They all shook their heads, they were happy to be with me, they hadn't an idea of what the word stranger meant. They took off briskly before me, I followed. Back up the stairs to the top of the hill. These children were students, just a few of the five thousand that Helicopter Swami supported. They led me to the cafeteria where they showed me off to their friends like a gold piece. We ate rice and dhal off banana leaves with our hands. I had no idea what I was doing there, but I knew there must be a reason, nothing Joan of Arc but it seemed I had to be there for a good reason or else I would not have come. I was welcome. Something I could never understand. I had indeed been the master of my time in the most insignificant way, I could not leave this way even if I tried, as if even if I were silent my life would be the same. I had a strange vision of this during an hallucination one time. There I was while time hit my face like hot wind. I never spoke but nothing changed, the whole life was absent of words but nothing changed.

I spent the day around my room writing little useless annals. It was always such a good time to write, I wish I were there now, writing not this but something else my imagination could conjure. Writing about real life is about as real as a dream. Yes, yes, Oscar. The day passed quickly and when the sun was heading off I made my way back up the stairs to find the main temple. A large marble edifice marked with countless carvings. I knew he was in there; I had been notified of his arrival but the bustling energy of the people around the temples outside made it evident. I removed my shoes and made my way in. I have worn the wrong clothes, I thought. Orange Thai pants and a black shirt. I must look like a follower of tantra or something, a test maybe. Do clothes really matter? Culturally, of course, but it couldn't be that shallow. As I stepped through two-story granite pillars the light went away and I found myself in a cold dark entrance leading to some stairs going up to the main room on a higher level.

Three great danes with red velvet collars blocked the stairs. They looked at me with pity. Their big brown eyes in those loose faces, they growled as I approached. I went for their heads with my right hand and rubbed the spot between each of their eyes. They were calm, they must have been a gift to the Swami. I had nothing, only my time. I walked past the dogs and up the stairs. In the center of the room stood an enormous Ganesha, I said hello to it in a monotone voice. I had seen him so often, more often than anything else. But would I have seen him if I hadn't known of his meaning? I walked around to the side and saw Helicopter Swami sitting in a big leather chair at the end of a long hallway lined with the same pillars I had walked past before. I started for him but was immediately stopped by two men who came out from the darkness with rifles. They spoke no English but insisted I go no further.

Helicopter Swami waved his hand and said something in Kannada. The two men backed off at once and motioned for me to walk down the way. When I made it to the side of the swami I put my hands together and bowed. He pointed to the floor beside him and told me to sit. I sat in lotus on the cold marble for a moment, and thought, The timeless nature of my situation, as one might feel in the mountains, the time does not exist, the made-up collective time forcefully shown by our egoistic historians and newsmen, the ego of mankind, our history, damn you Emerson for writing so true, but isn't it hard to find truth in words? Agreed, the true heart of man is universally understood, but to show this one must first master his understanding and control of the idiom. Some say if we study history, we shall know the future. Absurd, this nameless progression, look for the cyclical nature of civilization. Why? Man takes his hand for war on many accounts, war has always been a good history, war and items. The itemization of war goodies, the first records were of this. War from the mind birthed through the ego. Utopia could never exist unless all the participants were without ego. Hurray to the passive boycotted, the age of karma sum has begun. Silence was all it was with him after that, total silence in the mind. He was a calm man, his eyes never shuttered. It was a long while sitting before a few dozen children all dressed in bright pink robes entered the hall.

They, the virgin boys, sat in rows. One came with a harmonium, another with a set of tablas. Songs began, sweet sounds I'd never heard. They knew nothing else and wanted only to pleasure the ears of the man they held in such high regard. The sound of pure devotion and love, Louis Armstrong sang like that. He somehow kept the innocence within his words. Maybe with the end of seeing it all again comes the innocence, for the truth so much is driven by the sex mind that it is beyond the holder's understanding. How much do we need to see until it's over, how much must one desire? Maybe nothing, maybe it never has to begin, but if it didn't then it would never be. When the sounds stopped, the hall grew silent. The boys raised and one by one prostrated to the feet of their guru. They left without a sound.
"You want to go and learn something, yes?" He looked at me with a mischievous smile. "Well, yes, I would, I would like that." He pointed with his ring finger in some direction. "Then go to the hospital and stay, learn the language and maybe you will want to be doctor." I had never thought of becoming a doctor before, it seemed like a reasonable choice. "Of course. Tonight?" "Tomorrow morning at six, a van will pick you up where you are staying." It was time to leave him on that note, he could tell me nothing more. I gave him a bow and started on back to my room.

It was a well-built facility by local standerds a few years back, but you could see the wear in the paint from rain and smoke, years of use. The grounds were green and well-kept. In the back and sides were some partly built structures unfinished from lack of funds. Student dorms stood at the far sides of the property. I was left out in the front of the emergency room with a few young boys we had picked up along the way who were visiting friends. The driver, a good man, told me that I should find the administrative office and speak with the principal of the university. From there I could get a room and begin my time. I walked through the hospital halls smelling of iodine and alcohol. The locals curiously stared as I walked on through to the office. I was met by a secretary and sat on a leather couch in a waiting room. I asked her to teach me a few words in Kannada. I learned how to say hello, thank you, and where is the. She was a nice woman but she had no idea why I was there or who I was. You could see she thought it strange in the way her eyes moved when she looked away from mine.

An uncomfortable looking man with a toupee dressed in a suit too tight for his body came out from a door that was a two-way mirror, the principal. He waved me in past his body and gave me a seat in the front of his desk. "So why are you here my son?" So many times was I asked this same question. What was I supposed to say? I needed a joint, really. "I'm not sure exactly. I'd like to learn the language and go on rounds with the doctors to learn about medicine and see a bit of hospital life. Swami G said I should come." "And what do you do exactly?" "Professionally?" "Yes." "Nothing, sir, I am a student of the world at the moment, yes."

He looked at me, unsure of what to think, " Very well, then, we will put you in a room located in the special ward. You can stay there as long as you want and do as you like." It seemed he too thought I was strange. He tilted his head too often. The room was in a ward where most of the people were either passing away or severely injured, it was across from the ICU and the orthopedic ward. A group of nurses stationed at a desk beside the room greeted me. Three young women in their early twenties and a young man with the same years. In the room were two old hospital cots and a bathroom in the back with a toilet and a cold water faucet for showering.

"What are we, fucking dogs?" I stood in the center of my room with the stuff I had come to call my things. They were all strewn out on one of the medical cots. All the books I had brought along with me to make me feel safe and sometimes professorially calm knowing that I had great minds along with me and that at any moment I could open one up and feel less ignorant. I took the books and tore a few to pieces, pages flew around the room. "What am I doing here in this self inflicted limbo? Why am I not in Goa, or someplace with young people? I must have done this on purpose. Have I done this on purpose? Maybe I should get into some new drugs. Is there ever going to be enough time for any of us to think as long as we have already thought, but what more must we think about, or will we just eventually come to terms with the reality in which we've subconsciously placed ourselves, like the Talking Heads said. I lay back on the cold floor, closed my eyes, and looked back at the time behind me. It seemed I had done nothing but think, just as I was doing then, and as a matter of fact now as well. How inconvenient to contemplate the contemplative life for a lifetime. I cleaned up the room and got hold of myself. I was in the south of India in a hospital with a free room. "I must take this and do something productive and stimulating." I sat up, poring over the two questions I thought were quiet useless in the beginning: Who am I, and, What do I want to do? Questions with such endless questions within. Within is the *I* in what I want to do, and the doing in the *I* that I am. Not even the faintest spray of confusion. These pictures are to simple, I am truly fucked. But, here, so I see-saw.

Nothing and everything and this and that was going on and I forgot about the West a long time before, it seems like such a while; centuries of youth. I went and bought myself a few notebooks with faded blue covers from a simple place down the road, some pens as well. Night came with the moaning sounds from mouths of the wounded, sickly, and the ever-waiting elderly. I found little sleep that first night and stayed up writing, waiting for the next day to come just as it always did. I began a piece of fiction that I shan't resume, all sorts of shit happening, a self-exiled white man going to live a harsh and exciting life with Somali pirates. The captain of a crew he joins, soon after this white man's arrival, falls to the perils of simple conscience, yelling in the form of Marlow's devil and angel. Early the next day I went out into the halls and was met by that male nurse. We spent a few minutes discussing some simple Kannada that I wrote down in my fresh pages; he was a book-smart guy but could not understand why I was there. What an ignorant white man to think he would enjoy this place, moreover help. He was entranced with the idea of making it to the United States no matter what the cost; it was his golden dream and he treated me differently because of it, a lot of people did. They saw me and thought they knew so well what my mind was consumed with, they never asked, only interjected in a way that seemed impersonal, like speaking with a character in a movie only after you've memorized his lines, as if it would be that simple. I ate breakfast along with the doctors and they all stared at me. The looked uncomfortable and terrible like old dogs. No one spoke with me but the server of the foods, he gave me a smile and some extra chi. Satisfied by the curd and parathas, I returned to the room for a moment to collect my ideas for the time I was to spend with little planned.

Hold hands with me, hallucinate truth as we push on through with these grains upon these skins, one day we will meet the day with our true selves, there will be no difference between sleep and wake. The sun will shine even when the moon comes to soothe. The director of the hospital came by my room. His name was Sivani and he didn't care about anything beyond what it looked to be. He didn't want me there and saw me, as pointless but could not let down the word of his idol. He never asked me why I was there, but I think he may have thought that I was a mathematician from what I hear. He took me around the hospital and showed me where everything was and where I was to be, which was anywhere. He introduced me to a medical student in his final year of residency. I was to follow him on the morning rounds. He left me with this almost doctor and went back to his work. I had with me a blank book for writing notes on the medical processes and also to begin my further attempt at learning the local language. The guy was cynical and renounced the lower class, he spoke about poor killing each other in perfect English. A few with lost limbs, infections, a rape victim and the victim of fraudulent doctor. He thought I was stupid for coming. He made fun the first day we met and asked if I had learned any magic yet. After the rounds I should usually stop at the nurses' station, then I would go around the hospital speaking with patients roaming the halls. Lunch was taken and then a good nap. Afterward I went back out to wander around speaking with more people who worked in the hospital. I went over to the bus stop down the road and had a chi with a smoke and some workers. It was all time that went more slowly than anything I'd ever experienced. I spoke no more than a few words with the people on passing, to pass the time, they knew of a different world than I did. This all went on for some droppings of the sun. Until I met Dinesh, an ophthalmologist who had maintained this childish way, to breeze, I befriended him at once. We would spend afternoons discussing conservative mentalities and the shame that goes with them. He was a virgin and had no care in the world.

As I passed Sivani's office, he called me in. Sitting beside him was the man who looked after the Ganesha temple on the property beside the hospital. This pujari went by the name of F. He was to show me around and teach me some Kananda and Sanskrit. Sivani informed me if I might recite a classic slouch in traditional garb on a stage with Helicopter Swami in honor of the Indian Rotary Club and some Westerners that would come and run a free cleft pallet clinic for children. A few thousand would be there. I agreed and left the office with F pujari, and we walked the halls. "My country house," he was able to say with his limited English. He would come to my room whenever he could take me. He looked after some sugar cane and ragi.

Wake and dream alike, the light from day is same as night. Sitting on my bed before going off for rest. I sat atop my covers in lotus and thought of lucid dreaming. Conscious sleeping. The true controlled abstract. I set my own dream while awake and thought of it for a good while. I emptied it from my mind as I dozed off to sleep. Awake and fine. I do nothing on these long rolling green hills with you. The breeze came across my face, it was warm and I took off for the sky

Pujari F took me farther into the country, beyond burning coconut mounds and cane fields, to a dreary town with only a handful of huts tightly placed together. Old timers walk around. Kids play. The young men are gone off to work the cities. We walked the fields and chewed the cane; it was often he took me here. lead the lonely life and you may end up alone, you may always feel at home. Decide not to make to decisions and you'll probably be surprised. We were there on earth for no time and we had only lost our minds, but could we only think of being free with love. What was it that held us back from the mire of which I speak, the mud quick to steal your step, the calcification of the third eye?. There he is, the man I have been looking for, it is you. You master of ideas and lover of all that is. How long have you been sitting there? I can do nothing but you can do anything at all, put this book down and do something that emanates from yourself. Start an uprising and I shall join you, I shall walk with you across the desert. Write and I shall read, read and I shall listen. I am here for you only. These smiling eyes.

The group of Westerners came, I never spoke with them in passing, they were busy saving these children. They were saving these kids' lives. They did good things. All the children from surrounding villages that had suffered from any facial deformities were seen and operated on for free. To see a child in such a way, the weight upon them even before they have had time to make mistakes. And I with an unmarked face, the markless life. I am to be content in sitting on a porch for the rest of this show. I had all that I could ever have. These children, running games in the halls. When all the children were helped, a stage was set for a congratulatory event. I was to sing to them in honor of the swami and the doctors' work.

Testaments of the parents commenced, long joyous tears and the sobbing mouths. The gift of freedom, redemption to calm Before I walked on stage, the eldest looking doctor approached me. I wore a dhoti with a classic kurta top. "I have been meaning to ask what you are doing here young man." I laughed aloud. "Getting to know writing, and perhaps freeing ourselves from pointless future calamities,." He took wrapped mints from his pocket and handed one over. "I wish I had the time for these things, the vagabond student, we can all live vicariously through your experience, good luck to you." We are the vagabond students. All shall be revealed the true nature of life, and to the depths of searching, sleepless nights and fruitless company. Show your self before I end it all and lose patience with you. He walked back to the line of doctors. I rose from my seat on stage. I recited the Sanskrit slokah Pujari F had taught me out in the country. The people watched. When finished I prostrated before the man idol.

This day we drunkenly dance, swimming along. Fidel, the drop beat, long beat, deep bass, It all comes together. We are brothers. Do only as your heart demands. We are the quarry of the stone. the body, posture and breath, Failing vision, stealing from the poor, corruption in medicine. Countless sick people and people ready to leave this planet. Children taken by some force to the rough side. Bile. All of this, for me to be here with us and notice these fleeting notes upon the air. This farce so profound and true that when you're alone you watch the stars as a human man.

To go and live as the pauper and ration the rice and grow fat in the belly. To see the rain as enemy and friend but still be none the wiser for which you'd prefer. To know the sky and love its mood, a friend of the moons and the sun we walk along this high ridge. No more sit there to be one falling farouche. Back ground and round around again, then we'll see that we fly together at dark holding hands as our eyes fall from our heads and our minds escape the bloodless heart.

Before the sun. Dinesh saw me off. I boarded a bus on for Vishwa Shanti, Rama Mata's. I sat in the back row and rested my head against the glass. The white washed wildly roaming the watercolors. And the bus took me back to where she opened that door. A day early for the ceremonies. Nothing to say, nothing to make, and no place to go. What have we done? "Tea, Prem?" She smiled. I think for nothing, it's been such a time you know, it's so windy out here and I have only put my foot in the door, my little note. I'll be here with you to walk in them for a while. This room. And it is filled with these collected droves. Om & Prem

Yeah we'll breath here for a century in this always that we're present
Only pallidal swaths of always do help us turn to ferment
In this yet madness, smack game Brando's, the willing bogies smoked.
Demented open masses bathing John Doe, even after he's gone broke
This movement without meter, all the gusto without heirs
.We shall breathe now for a culture, in this second we are here.

www.ingramcontent.com/pod-product-compliance
Lightning Source LLC
Chambersburg PA
CBHW071959040426
42447CB00009B/1402